A Place Where the Sea Remembers

and Related Readings

McDougal Littell
A HOUGHTON MIFFLIN COMPANY

Evanston, Illinois   *Boston*   *Dallas*

Acknowledgments

Coffee House Press and Simon & Schuster: *A Place Where the Sea Remembers* by Sandra Benítez. Copyright © 1993 by Sandra Benítez. Originally appeared in a hardcover edition published by Coffee House Press. A trade paperback edition published by Scribner Paperback Fiction is also available. *A Place Where the Sea Remembers* has been reprinted herein by permission of the publishers, Coffee House Press and Simon & Schuster.

Farrar, Straus & Giroux, Inc.: "Night," from *The Blue Estuaries: Poems 1923–1968* by Louise Bogan. Copyright © 1968 by Louise Bogan. Reprinted by permission of Farrar, Straus & Giroux, Inc.

Viking Penguin: "All day I hear the noise of waters," from *Collected Poems* by James Joyce. Copyright 1918 by B.W. Huebsch, Inc., 1927, 1936 by James Joyce, 1946 by Nora Joyce. Used by permission of Viking Penguin, a division of Penguin Books USA Inc.

Arte Público Press: "Talking to the Dead" by Judith Ortiz Cofer is reprinted with permission from the publisher of *Silent Dancing: A Partial Remembrance of a Puerto Rican Childhood* (Houston: Arte Público Press—University of Houston, 1990). "Paciencia" by Judith Ortiz Cofer is reprinted with permission from the publisher of *The Americas Review*, Vol. 16, No. 2 (Houston: Arte Público Press—University of Houston, 1988).

Continued on page 197.

Cover illustration by Pat Dypold.

ISBN 0-395-83361-2

5 6 7 8 9 QNT 04 03 02 01

Contents

A Place
Where
the Sea
Remembers

Sandra Benítez

Chapter 1

Remedios

La Curandera
(curandera, n.f. healer)

Remedios, *la curandera,* stands at the edge of the sea. The old healer is weary, a result, in part, of the countless times she has cocked her head in the direction of someone's story. Remedios knows the town's stories. Just as the sea, as their witness, knows them, too.

Remedios looks out over the deep. Tucked under an arm is the swordfish beak that is one of her prized possessions. She has owned it for many years. Usually she keeps the sword in her hut, on her altar, *la mesa santa.* Not today. Today she has brought the sword to the sea because it signifies the waters and the mighty fish that live there. She has brought it because *el pico de pez espada* helps her find those who have drowned.

Today Remedios awaits the one blue wave that will bring a corpse to shore. The body we wait for, she thinks, the sea will yield up. Today. Tomorrow. The sea cannot be rushed. The others wring their hands, hold their breaths on the far side of the crag, at the place where the river joins the sea. But not Remedios.

El pico has led her to this spot, and it is here she'll keep her vigil.

Gathering her long dark skirt between her legs, Remedios squats on the shore. She lays *el pico* across her lap. Around her neck is the cord from which her medicine pouch hangs. The pouch rests directly over her heart and contains the secret talismans that fortify and empower her. Remedios spreads a palm over the little pouch, then reaches for the line of foamy brine rippling toward her. In the biting honesty of salt, the sea makes her secrets known to those who care to listen. She touches a finger to her tongue and the stories come.

The sea remembers. So it is the sea retells.

Chapter 2

Candelario Marroquín

El Ensaladero
(ensaladero, n.m. salad-maker)

On the day after his promotion to salad-maker, Candelario Marroquín painted the door of his house a robin's egg blue. The color blue was an obsession for him. Since his youth he had found comfort in the special blueness of new mornings. The azure stars that edged Our Lady's mantle inspired him almost always to pray. And the glinting cobalt of the sea produced in him such excitement that he was forced at times to turn his back on it. "When it comes to blue," his wife Chayo said, "who can understand him?" She was away when he began to paint the door. She had taken a basketful of paper flowers to the beach in hopes of selling them to tourists.

Candelario worked at his door in an act of quiet celebration. Each stroke of the brush soothed him and left him more at peace. Now that he had advanced from a mere waiter to the salad-maker, he would wear the cummerbund and the stiff bow tie. His small, thick body would look distinguished and important in the room where so many dined. Salary and tips would increase too. In the years since they had married, Candelario and Chayo had worked hard and earned little. It was the way of life here in Santiago. When he lived behind the mountain range that stretched all the way to Mexico City, Candelario had tended the bulls that later would be sent to fight. His work had been brutal, but there was always enough to eat and, most times, enough pesos left over for a glass or two of pulque in the cantina.

Since marrying he had become a much more serious man. At Chayo's insistence he had given up the bulls for a more tranquil life. He did not drink anymore, for the pesos he made at the restaurant would not allow such indulgence. Chayo, too, felt the weight of life's difficulties. The tourists were sometimes so clever at bargaining that she could never count on much from the sale of her bouquets. But all that was in the past. Now that he was the salad-maker, their lot was sure to improve.

It was a good day for painting. The sun was high and there was hardly a breeze. Candelario Marroquín stepped back to admire his handiwork. The enamel had taken smoothly to the metal door. At the top, where the paint was nearly dry, the door reflected the brightness of the morning. I can thank the *patrón* for this, he thought. Don Gustavo del Norte owned the restaurant in which Candelario worked. Don Gustavo was a large man, soft-muscled but surprisingly quick in manner. He had opened his establishment not long after moving to Santiago. Five months before, he had left Guadalajara, where he had lived for many years. There he had owned a glass factory in the nearby village of Tlaquepaque. Candelario Marroquín had never been so far away and could not himself imagine a village spilling over with tiny shops, all dependent on the whims of tourists. He had asked Hortencio, the wine steward, about this. Hortencio had worked for don Gustavo in the glass factory, and he knew about merchants and about the ways of a city like Guadalajara.

"Why did don Gustavo leave one business for another?" Candelario asked. "Doesn't Don Gustavo know more about glassmaking than about food?"

Hortencio had not answered either question. Instead, he had shrugged his shoulders and continued to polish the silver cup that dangled from the chain he wore around his neck.

Candelario squatted to paint the bottom third of the door. It was not for him to question the *patrón's* motives. Don Gustavo was a man of clever ideas. It was his most recent belief that the tourists of Santiago deserved other things to eat than tacos and enchiladas. Just last week he had told Candelario that he would offer something different, feature some specialty for which the restaurant might become known. He had settled on the Caesar salad. Don Gustavo himself had instructed Candelario on how to make it. "For a perfect Caesar," the *patrón* said, "the correct bowl is essential." He had brought just the one from Guadalajara. It was wide at the base and lacquered black with squat, bowed sides. "You must prepare this salad with a flair," don Gustavo said. Candelario Marroquín had taken to this requirement. Secretly, he was proud of his ways in the bullring. Now he would transfer his bravura to the salad cart.

"We have anchovies," Candelario said as he finished up the painting. He mimicked don Gustavo's instructions, wrinkling his nose at the acrid smell of the paint. "Then comes the mustard, then the lemons." The sun now struck the door with an intensity that made him squint. "We have the eggs and then the romaine." Candelario Marroquín pictured his cart: the narrow side-racks holding bottles and small shakers, the bottom shelf stacked high with plates, on the rims of which were stenciled delicate birds the color of his door.

Candelario propped his brush in the paint can and sat on the ground, his back against the wall of the house. He wiped his forehead with the back of a hand and glanced down the dry riverbed that fronted the house and led all the way to the sea. In the dry season the arroyo was used as a road, and now Chayo strode up it on her way back from the beach. Chayo's sister, Marta, came along too. Marta was fifteen, four years younger than Chayo; each had the same dark mole, high on the cheekbone under the left eye. Candelario Marroquín noted that Marta's pregnancy was not yet visible and he was glad of it. When her condition became apparent, there would be more than enough time for the town to talk.

That Chayo and he were childless he was certain the town already discussed. It perturbed him to think that his and Chayo's names could lie on the lips of so many. He often asked himself if it were pity that people felt for them. "Poor Chayo," he imagined people saying. "In these two years there could have been two babies." Candelario Marroquín bristled at the thought. He had no use for people's pity. He himself felt divided about his wife's condition. He knew that while having sons would show him to be the man he truly was, more mouths for him to feed would be a considerable burden.

Now Chayo and Marta approached Candelario. When she saw the blue door, Chayo rolled her eyes. "It's not surprising," she said.

Candelario said nothing, but he was pleased nonetheless at his wife's observation. The three went to sit under the lime tree growing at the edge of the yard, for they could not enter the house until the paint dried on the door handle.

"I sold all my flowers today," Chayo said, tucking

her skirt neatly under her legs. "One tourist wanted my basket, so I sold that too."

"She made sixteen thousand pesos," Marta said.

"It is a fortunate day," Candelario replied, a wave of contentment washing over him. Of late it seemed that his life had turned around. Things were going right again. "We will buy more paint with the money. Now I can paint the inside of the house." Candelario and Chayo's house had only one room and one window. Their marriage bed sat under the window, one side against the wall. The furniture had belonged to Chayo's mother. "When I'm gone, I wish you to have it," she had said.

"In a few days the doctor will be in town," Marta said. She smoothed her dress over her belly. "If I'm to put an end to my situation, it must be done soon. Time is running out."

What's this? Candelario asked himself. He usually paid no attention to the women when they talked. It was his observation that, in one way or another, women always spoke of life or death. Candelario Marroquín preferred more practical subjects. Today, however, he paid close attention to what the two said.

"I don't know if it's the right thing," Chayo said.

"It's right," Marta replied. Although young, she had a determination and intensity of manner rare among the girls of Santiago. "It's right because Roberto did this when I did not want it." She struck her belly with a clenched fist. "If I have this child, I will hate it for all my life. I will hate this child like I hate Roberto."

Chayo said, "Have the child. Tía Fina will help you raise it." Marta lived with tía Fina, the women's aunt, in a rooming house in Santiago.

"Tía Fina can't do it. With her heart like it is, she can't look after children. Besides, I don't want to have a baby. I want to see the doctor when he comes. *El doctor* is the only one to help me."

Chayo said, "I have heard of infection, of death, resulting from what you want."

"*El doctor* comes from Guadalajara. He has learned many things in the city. He will not harm me."

"If you do this, you will harm your soul," Chayo said.

Marta wrenched a handful of grass from the ground. "Perhaps souls can be mended," she said, allowing the grass blades to slip like rain through her fingers.

Chayo shook her head. "Padre Mario will condemn this."

"*El cura* cannot see into my heart. It is not for him to judge."

For a moment the two fell silent and Candelario thought that the subject was closed and that it was Marta's straight forwardness that had ended the conversation, but then Chayo asked, "What about Remedios? Surely *la curandera* could tell you what to do."

Marta turned her gaze up the arroyo. "I don't need the healer. I know best what's good for me."

"And the doctor?" Chayo asked. "How much does he charge?"

"One hundred thousand pesos," Marta said. "I have money saved, but I still need more. If I made enough, I'd pay for this myself." Marta cleaned rooms in the best hotel in town.

Candelario creased a lime leaf in half and let its essence escape. He rubbed the leaf's edge against his fingers dotted blue with paint. One hundred thousand pesos. If tips were good, it would take him weeks to earn that amount.

"Are you sure of the cost?" Chayo asked.

"As sure as I can be," Marta said. "Luz told me." Luz worked in the hotel with Marta. She lived in the same rooming house where Marta and her aunt lived.

"*Yo soy el ensaladero,*" Candelario Marroquín said. "Have the child. Chayo and I will take it." He had not known that he would say this. Where had the idea come from? Could he take it back?

"Cande," Marta said, her face going soft. She looked over at her sister whose eyes had widened and who was staring at Candelario. Marta turned to look at him too. "Cande, are you sure?"

Candelario Marroquín squared his shoulders to show a little earnestness. "Now that I'm the salad-maker, we will have money to raise your child." What else could he say? He had made the offer, and it is a man's duty to honor what he says. He did not question his own decisions, no matter how hastily they were made. With the bulls, a moment of uncertainty could get you a sharp horn in the side. He looked at his wife but detected in her face only a slight pallor that caused the mole under her eye to appear darker.

Marta lightly touched her sister's shoulder. "Chayo, will you really do this for me?"

"Cande says so, therefore it will be done."

Marta said, "I will hate the child less if you raise it."

* * *

Some months later, very late at night, Candelario Marroquín arrived home from work. He placed his cummerbund and bow tie on the dresser and, because he was not sleepy, he opened the front door and stood there, looking out. Across the arroyo the little houses that stood in a row appeared like chalky bundles in the moonlight. The odor of wood smoke left behind from the day's labors drifted in, and Candelario savored this sign of his neighbors' industriousness.

"I had a dream," Chayo said from their bed. She had been asleep when Candelario came in, but now she was propped up against the wall, her legs drawn up against her chest. Her long hair hung loose and fell like a dark mantilla over the tucks and gathers in her nightgown. She told him of the dream from which he'd awakened her.

She stood at the edge of the sea. Rhythmically the waves reached her, wetting first her toes, and then her ankles and finally her calves. She looked out to sea and tossed a sapphire-tinted flower onto each new cresting wave. She dreamed of watching her paper blossoms ride out to meet the sharp line of the horizon.

"Do you think it was a bad dream, Cande?" she asked.

"How can it be," he replied, "when there was so much blue in it?"

After a time, as the two lay nestled in bed, Candelario whispered, "Don Gustavo will have important guests tomorrow. The doctor will come, the one with the clinic, the one from Guadalajara." A cool breeze entered through the window and Chayo pulled their blanket more securely around them. "The doctor and his wife are friends of don Gustavo. He is eager to impress them."

Chayo was silent for a bit, but then she said, "He is the one Marta would have gone to. He is the one who helps the women."

Candelario had had some time to think how their life would change once Marta's baby arrived. Over the months a new thought had come to him. Could the presence of the child induce Chayo's womb to yield him up a son? He would love Marta's child for that. He knew without question that he would. In a moment of clarity, he allowed himself to look ahead. He pictured himself, in some hazy future time, the head of a family of many sons. He imagined his children eyeing with admiration his cummerbund and bow tie. Candelario sighed contentedly. "I am a fortunate man," he said. "We do not need the doctor's help." Chayo's body stiffened and she turned away and he blamed the gesture on the coolness in the room. "I'll make the Caesar for them," he added. "It'll bring a good tip."

"And if they don't like the salad?" Chayo asked. "What will happen then?"

"You must not worry," he said. "If they are hard to please, I will enlighten them as I always do with the fussy ones." In the months that he'd been salad-maker, Candelario had received some complaints about the salad, but always he had managed to ease misunderstandings. No need to involve the *patrón* in this, he'd thought. Candelario explained to the guests that this was don Gustavo's Caesar and as such it was special and very different. Candelario himself knew how different the salad was: all those greens coated with mustard and beaten egg. On one occasion he had tasted the dish and vowed never to again. How can people eat this? he had asked himself. But then, who was he to question the foods the rich enjoyed? Didn't they eat mashed potatoes and that concoction named yogurt? Candelario gave a little shudder at the thought.

Chayo said, "The doctor and his wife. They are rich. They will drink imported wine. Hortencio's tip will be greater than yours."

"It is not important," Candelario said. "I only wish for my share." He turned and pressed himself against his wife's back, taking in the musky fragrance that was always caught in her hair.

On the following evening Candelario Marroquín watched as the visitors were seated by don Gustavo himself at a table with the best view of the sea. Candelario stood off to the side and waited for the snap of the *patrón's* fingers. When he was called to service, he rolled his cart toward the guests. "Good evening," he said to the couple. He laid linen napkins across each of their laps. Don Gustavo hovered behind the doctor, a middle-aged man whose large belly kept him at a slight angle from the table. The doctor's wife was thin and very tanned; there were thick gold bracelets around her wrists. Long ago, Candelario had observed that women who were rich seemed to struggle to be thin. It was a curious thing. To have food in abundance and yet to choose to eat little.

"We'll have the Caesar," the woman said to Candelario. "It's a favorite, and for me, it'll be a meal."

The doctor said, "In addition, I'll have the beef steak and a potato." Turning to don Gustavo, he said, "But first, won't you join us for a glass of champagne, Gustavo? María Elena and I would like to toast your new business venture." With an upturned hand, he made a sweeping gesture to point out the room.

"Jumping from glassmaking into the restaurant business seems to me an interesting move," the wife said. The discs that dangled from her bracelets struck each other and made a happy sound.

"An interesting move full of hard work," don Gustavo replied. Turning to the doctor, he added, "It will be my pleasure to join you for a glass, but only if you're my guests." He sat, ordered the wine from Hortencio, who stood by the table, and then clapped at Candelario to begin the salad.

"I'll watch him make the Caesar," the woman said.

Smiling down at the cart, Candelario laid two anchovies in the bottom of the bowl. With the back of a fork he mashed them into a paste. Because the woman was watching, he put some style into the mashing.

"I passed the clinic today," don Gustavo said.

"There was a line stretching out into the street. You're a very busy man."

"When we come here, I don't see him until nightfall," the doctor's wife said. "I spend my day at the beach."

Candelario looked up to see her take a sip from her water glass. She used a napkin to dab the corners of her bright red mouth. Candelario dipped a tablespoon into the mustard jar and dolloped three spoonfuls into the bowl. He mixed the mustard with the anchovy paste, pleased that the *patrón* could see how faithfully he executed the recipe.

Candelario glanced up again for a quick check of the table and was disappointed to note he'd lost his audience. Hortencio had appeared with the long-legged ice bucket. He made a show of uncorking the champagne, and poured the wine into three tulip-shaped glasses.

"You do so much for the women of Santiago," don Gustavo said after the doctor had made a toast and Hortencio had gone on to another table. "So many babies would not survive but for your clinic."

"It's the least I can do," the doctor replied, settling himself more comfortably in the chair. "You know how successful my practice is in Guadalajara. I've been very lucky. I come here periodically to provide for those who can't provide for themselves. When life is good, it's only right to give."

"The people need to be educated," don Gustavo said. "Some are filthy. Their children are filthy. It's no wonder so many sicken and die."

Candelario Marroquín thrust his fork deep into the flesh of half a lemon. He squeezed its juice into the bowl. *Educate them.* How often had he heard these words? It shamed him that at twenty-eight he could not read, that the only writing he could do was to scratch out his name. If he were to be educated, who would teach him? How easily the rich spoke of solutions. How untroubled and simple their lives seemed to be.

"It's not always the people's fault for the filth that surrounds them," the doctor said. "Filth is a symptom of the corruption in our society. It's a disease that flourishes in poverty. I try to do my part. I wish I could do more."

His wife said, "You do much for the people, Federico." Turning to don Gustavo she said, "He delivers babies practically for free. If therapeutic abortions are indicated, he does those equally as cheap."

Candelario broke two eggs into the bowl just as he'd been taught to do. He followed with keen interest the bent of the conversation.

Don Gustavo made a clucking sound. "Abortions," he said, lowering his voice and glancing quickly around the room before turning back to the doctor. "You know abortions are illegal."

"My dear Gustavo," the doctor said, "of course they are. María Elena is very precise about medical terms. Perhaps you'd feel more comfortable if she referred to therapeutic abortions as terminations of pregnancy. These are legal, you know, if there is good cause."

Candelario whipped the eggs into a froth. His fork clicked against the sides of the bowl.

"And what would you consider good cause?" don Gustavo asked.

"Jeopardy of the mother's life due to the fetus," the doctor replied. "Certain deformities of the fetus."

"*Violación*," the woman said.

"Rape?" don Gustavo said.

"In my estimation," the doctor said, "rape is a legitimate reason for this procedure."

"Both the law and the Church would quarrel with

you on that," don Gustavo said.

"My dear man," the doctor replied, "I am used to quarreling with the Church."

Candelario set his jaw. He could feel the cords in his neck straining against his bow tie.

"But how can you know it's rape?" don Gustavo asked. "Surely you don't believe all the women who cry rape."

Candelario placed his fork upon the cart. His face was hot. He wiped the palms of his hands against his apron.

"And who would you have him believe?" the doctor's wife asked. "Do you think Federico has the luxury of interviewing the men in question?"

"María Elena," don Gustavo said with a little laugh, "you sound so North American."

The woman replied, "No, no. It's not that. These are the 1980s, you understand."

After a pause, don Gustavo asked, "You do this free of charge?"

"I charge only a modest fee," the doctor said.

"He charges twenty thousand pesos," the woman said. "That is an affordable amount for any woman to pay."

Candelario took two plates from the bottom rack of the cart and placed them next to the salad bowl. He gave the salad a final toss. The romaine leaves glistened with eggy coating. Twenty thousand pesos. He should have known. Why had Marta listened to her friend, Luz? Luz was excitable, and she was a dreamer, and who could trust a person like that? Candelario served each guest, dusted the salads with cheese and then rolled the cart to the side of the room. He wished fate had not placed him at the table. He wished that, months ago, he had not been a party to the change in Marta's life.

Soy el ensaladero, he reminded himself. I do not

need to fear the future. He went into the kitchen to select the greens for his next salad.

Candelario was at the refrigerator when don Gustavo rushed up.

"There's a problem at the doctor's table. It's the salad. They can't eat it. What have you done?"

"How can it be?" Candelario said. "It was made as it should be. I must speak with them." He reached to center his bow tie and then he hurried into the dining room, the *patrón* at his heels.

"May I be of service," Candelario said to the doctor and his wife. Each had their salad before them, the woman's looked untouched, the doctor's had barely been eaten.

"It's nothing," the woman said. "We told Gustavo that it was nothing."

"None of that, none of that," the *patrón* said with a shake of his hand. "A mistake has obviously been made. If you can't eat the salad, there has been some mistake."

"Well," the doctor said, "there is no garlic here and no oil." He lightly touched the edge of his plate.

"There is a reason for this," Candelario said, stealing a quick look at the *patrón*.

"I'm sorry," the wife said, "but it's just too eggy for me." She pushed her plate into the middle of the table.

Don Gustavo addressed Candelario, "Explain what you have done."

Candelario nodded and he informed the guests about don Gustavo's Caesar. He thrust out his thick chest and he told of the anchovies and the mustard and then the lemon and finally the eggs. "Oh, I ask your pardon," he said. "I meant to say, finally the cheese."

There was a silence after the litany. The doctor and his wife looked at each other. Don Gustavo looked around him. Other guests had stopped eating and were now intent on what occurred at this table.

Taking all this in, Candelario felt a rush of foreboding. "I make the salad as I was taught," he said. "Perhaps there are many ways to prepare it, but I prepare it the only way I know. I follow the recipe just as it was explained to me." Candelario knew that his words were hurried. He should slow down, be more thorough, but panic drove his thoughts and propelled him to explain, to try to shake them all from this misjudgment.

"I'd like to know who it was that taught this *indio*," don Gustavo said. "Who has heard of a Caesar without garlic, without oil." He puckered his lips in distaste. "It's nothing but ridiculous."

"There should be croutons, too," the woman blurted and then clapped a hand over her mouth.

"Of course, croutons," the *patrón* said.

The doctor rose from his chair. "Gustavo, for the love of God," he said. "You make much of nothing. This is not important."

"It's important to me," don Gustavo said, striking his chest. Turning to Candelario, he added, "I will see you in the kitchen."

Candelario was on his way down the hall when don Gustavo caught up with him.

"Do you understand what you have done?" the *patrón* said. He reached into his coat pocket and extracted a handkerchief and mopped his face. "The doctor and his wife are friends of mine. They are two very important people. You have embarrassed me in front of them."

"But Don Gustavo, I did nothing wrong."

The *patrón's* face was very red. "You made the salad and they could not eat it. Everyone in the restaurant saw they could not eat it."

"But it was your salad, Don Gustavo. It was you . . ."

"*¡Basta!* I will not have a salad-maker who cannot

make salads. Tomorrow, *indio de la chingada*, you can look elsewhere for work."

*　*　*

Candelario Marroquín extinguished the candles that graced the tables of don Gustavo's restaurant. Some candles he blew out, others he smothered with the tips of two fingers. He welcomed the quick pain. It was a distraction from the humiliation he'd suffered earlier, from the humiliation he still felt at having to finish out the evening before collecting his pay. When he reached the last candle, his fingertips were numb. Still he touched them to his tongue as if the gesture would make a difference.

Candelario placed each chair upside down upon its table. He swept the floor and mopped the tile until it darkened to the color of wet stones. He switched off the lights and looked out to the sea. The sea did not cheer him. Don Gustavo's words echoed in his head like pounding waves.

He went into the kitchen. Hortencio was near the sink. His face looked pale in the eerie glow of fluorescent lighting.

"Where is Don Gustavo?" Candelario Marroquín asked.

"He has left. If you are finished, I have your pay."

"I am finished."

Candelario Marroquín untied the cummerbund from around his waist, the bow tie from around his neck. He placed both on the table. Silently, he picked up his money and stepped out into a starless night.

Chapter 3

Remedios Elementales: Tierra

(tierra, n.f. earth)

Remedios's hut sits at the top of the hill. It faces the road, its back to the sea that lies off in the distance. The hut has two windows, brush walls, a woven-palm roof. A pair of *nogales* offer some shade. Beyond the trees a plot of corn flourishes; off to the side, the cacti catch the full brunt of the sun: San Pedro and cholla, aloe and agave.

The hut is simply furnished. There is a cot and a dresser, a table and chairs. Grasses and herbs hang drying from *vigas* stretched across the ceiling. There is *romero, salvia, hierbabuena, helecho macho, manzanilla, cola de caballo, malva,* and *siempre viva,* to name some.

La mesa santa, Remedios's altar, dominates the middle of the hut. The altar is spread with a white linen cloth. Four candles are aligned in the four sacred directions and define the altar's space. Earth and sea have offered up gifts for *la mesa santa:* the cloven hoof of a deer, the beak of a swordfish. Snake and owl stones, river and lake stones, sea and wind stones. Triton shells, oyster shells, snail and pearl shells. On the altar, too, is the clay bat bestowed on Remedios by don Cipriano, her mentor. He granted it to her to commemorate her spiritual rebirth.

Along one edge of *la mesa santa*, statues of sacred figures are lined up: San Rafael Arcángel, La Virgen Dolorosa, San Martín de Porres, El Santo Niño de Atocha. In the middle of the altar, Jesús Crucificado.

Artemisa and cedar bundles are bunched in a rush basket. In a sooty bowl, fat nuggets of copal. There are ears of yellow corn, a shallow dish of *cal*. A wooden pipe, black tobacco in a pouch. A red-clay whistle she molded herself when she was eight from the muds surrounding her home.

Chiseled-edged flints and polished crystals lie against the altar cloth. A hollow gourd-rattle. An amber jar of scented water collects the rays of the sun. And there are magpie, hummingbird and eagle feathers, rabbit bones, lizard and snake skins. There is the desiccated, iridescent husk of a dragonfly.

Remedios stands at *la mesa santa*, her bare feet planted on the cool earth floor of the hut. She lights the candles, beginning with the one representing the east. She lights the artemisa smudge-stick, drawing the sweet smoking bundle up over her head, down along her arms, her legs, up toward her heart, the true centering place. As she smudges, she invokes the Mother, the Father, the Great Spirit, turning to the sacred directions as she prays. Though she is old, her voice is deep and resonant. She takes up the smooth gourd-rattle and chants: I am she who knows. I am bone woman. I am bird woman. I am she-woman. He-woman. I am moon woman. Sun woman. Star woman. I am she who weeps. She who bleeds. I am she who speaks. I am the woman who cries out. I am the silent woman. I am earth woman. Fire woman. I am water woman. Air woman. I am she who keeps. She who holds. I am she who heals. *Soy Remedios, la curandera.* I am she who knows. *Soy la que sabe.*

Chapter 4

Fulgencio Llanos

El Fotógrafo
(fotógrafo, n.m. photographer)

Fulgencio Llanos hurried around the corner just in time to see the bus pull away from the curb. He yelled out, but the bus did not stop. It rumbled off toward the highway, leaving behind a cloud of diesel fumes that set Fulgencio to coughing. "*¡Chinga!*" he exclaimed, hiking up the wooden tripod tucked under his arm. That was the last bus home.

Fulgencio set his tripod down on the sidewalk. He laid down the large, square valise that held his camera and the assortment of props that over the years he had diligently collected for his photo sittings.

In the valise, too, was the film he'd shot only yesterday of El Santo, the masked wrestler who was the toast of all Mexico. The photographs were sure to change Fulgencio's life. Next week, he planned a trip to Mexico City, where he would stride into the offices of *La Tribuna,* the newspaper known for carrying articles on the wrestler's matches and his exploits. "I have uncovered El Santo's identity," Fulgencio would announce, and for a stiff price and the certainty of celebrity, he would provide the newspaper with the photographs showing the wrestler frolicking in the surf at an out-of-the-way beach without the full face mask that was his signature.

Fulgencio pushed his gray felt hat back on his forehead. He looked down the road to see the bus turn onto the highway and disappear behind the side of the cantina at the end of the street. He spat on the sidewalk and took a handkerchief from his trouser pocket and mopped his face with it. He would have to find a ride. Santiago, the town that for now he called home, was nearly thirty kilometers away. It was almost six o'clock. He stuffed the handkerchief back into his pocket, noting the way the sun spread its waning light over the dirt-packed street and up the smudged adobe wall of the cantina.

Fulgencio was weary and hungry. He was bent on reaching home and the bowl of soup and plateful of shrimp he customarily ordered in Lupe Bustos's *comedor*. From time to time, throughout the afternoon, his thoughts had turned to Lupe and how the sight of her strutting about her eating place was all he needed to feel revived.

Fulgencio gave the side of his valise a soft kick. He should have left doña Elvira Cantos's house a little earlier. But no, he had sat with the woman for what seemed like a thousand hours in the stuffy front room with the severe furniture, drinking the weak lemonade she offered, struggling to keep his eyes from settling on the dark stubble that sprouted from around her lips, telling her that though she was a woman of maturity, she was still a beauty and such beauty should, without a doubt, be captured by his camera. "You know the camera does not lie," he told her, and she raised a fat hand to her mouth and giggled behind it, rolling her eyes that were as small and moist as a pigeon's. "*Ay, Señor Llanos*," she cooed, "*cómo exagera.*" She poured him another glass of lemonade.

In the end, he drank three glasses, and despite the feat, she had still not agreed to sit for him. "Come back tomorrow and we'll discuss the matter further," she had said, grunting softly as she rose from her settee.

Out on the sidewalk, Fulgencio's bladder felt the weight of all that lemonade. I'm getting too old for this, he thought, determined to never set foot in the hag's house again. He was not yet fifty, and for more years than he cared to recall he had made his living roaming the Mexican countryside, photographing men, women and children, the events and possessions in their lives.

It was not easy to live his life: there was the constant travel, the heft and tug of his equipment as he went from town to town. And there was all that conversation to be made, all that nudging and cajoling. No, it was not an easy task he faced each day. It took hard work and subtle inducements to convince people that what they possessed, what they experienced, was deserving of a photograph. "Photographs," he was fond of saying, "photographs properly sized, properly framed, are precious and rightful additions to any home."

Of course, times had gone from bad to worse and money was scarce, and so his forms of persuasion had, by necessity, grown more and more inventive. It was draining to have to be so imaginative, so pleasant, when if truth be told, there were days when his heart was not in it. But that was all behind him. After his trip to the capital, his life would be changed. He thanked the stars that yesterday had placed him on the beach with his camera and his telescopic lens.

Fulgencio Llanos lifted his hat and scratched his head before patting the hat back in place again. He reached for his tripod and tucked it back under his arm. He yanked up his valise and started across the street. He would go into the cantina to relieve his bladder. Then a quick *cerveza* before trudging to the highway to flag down a ride.

He was halfway through his Dos Equis when the gringo came in. The man was tall and, though somewhat slender, seemed to fill the room when he stepped through the door. The buzz of conversation that pervaded the cantina diminished when he came in, but the gringo seemed not to notice. He walked over to the bar and sat on the stool next to Fulgencio's.

"*Una Bohemia,*" the gringo said to the bartender.

Fulgencio took a long swallow of beer. He kept a watch on the newcomer by means of the mirror hanging over the back of the bar. Others in the room soon lost interest. Not Fulgencio. Where there's a gringo, there's usually a car, he thought. He envisioned himself riding in comfort all the way to Lupe Bustos's *comedor*. He pictured Lupe watching him step out of a long, sleek Cadillac. The bartender came up and set a Bohemia in front of the gringo.

Fulgencio examined the man reflected in the mirror. He wore a straw hat with a deep crease in its crown. A red bandanna was wrapped around its circumference. He looks like a cowboy, Fulgencio thought. Fulgencio knew gringo cowboys from the movies. They travel astride horses, but not this man. This one must own a Cadillac, parked just outside the door. Fulgencio tried to settle on the color of the car. Black, he thought. No, red. It would be red.

"Are you from here?" the gringo asked abruptly. He spoke the simple, direct Spanish of gringos who live just north of the border.

Fulgencio turned to the man. "Are you talking to me, Señor?"

"Yes, to you, but don't use *señor*. I am Jim. Jaime."

He extended a hand.

Fulgencio took the man's hand. "*Soy Fulgencio.*"

The gringo was friendly, but this was not surprising—most gringos were friendly. What was surprising was the size of his hand, the power in his grip, and the fact that he wore his hair in a thick, blond ponytail that lay just under the back brim of his hat. Fulgencio wondered why he had not noticed this before. He turned back to his beer and took a gulp. Was that an earring gleaming in the gringo's earlobe? Fulgencio shook his head. He thought, The man is not a cowboy, he is a *heepee*. It had been some time since Fulgencio had seen one. He remembered, many years back, when hippies were a common sight in Mexico. There had been a movie popular then about a band of them traveling across the country in a dilapidated van. The red Cadillac parked in Fulgencio's mind underwent a sudden transformation.

"So, Fulgencio, are you from here?"

"No, Señor, I am from Santiago. It is down the road." Fulgencio hooked a thumb in the direction of home.

"I'm going to Santiago," the gringo said. "Actually to Manzanillo. That's not far from Santiago."

"No. It's not far." That *was* an earring the gringo was wearing. Fulgencio remembered that in the movie, the hippies had not owned a car. They had not owned much of anything. They'd sent their girls to stand at the edge of highways so that cars would stop for them. Fulgencio downed the last of his beer. This gringo probably doesn't own a car, he thought. He's probably being friendly to get a ride from me. Fulgencio felt tired again.

"You are a photographer?" the gringo said. "You have a tripod." He pointed to it leaning against the bar.

"*Sí. Soy fotógrafo,*" Fulgencio said, adding nothing

more. It was time to get going. He had wasted enough time talking to someone who did not own a car. If he was lucky, there was still enough daylight left to go out to the highway and flag down a ride.

"*¿Su cámara?*"

Fulgencio placed his foot on the valise resting on the floor next to the stool. "*Aquí.*"

"*¿Una Minolta? ¿Una Nikon?*"

Fulgencio shook his head. "*Una Speed Gráfica.*" He stepped down from the stool. "Well, Señor Jaime, I must be going. I have to find a ride. Soon it will be dark." There. The truth was out. He had no car. That was sure to put an end to all the friendliness.

The gringo said, "I have a car. You can ride with me."

"¡Ah!" Fulgencio exclaimed and smiled broadly. Well, well, he thought. "Do you have room for my equipment?"

The gringo nodded. "*Mi carro es muy grande.*"

They paid for their beers and Fulgencio picked up his things. The two went out to the street. Parked by the curb was an old Ford station wagon. It had high, wide wheel wells and a broad flaring hood. The sides of the car, and even the back, were covered with panels of creamy yellow wood. Inside, red-checkered curtains were drawn at the side windows.

The gringo walked over to the front passenger's door. "This is Woody," he grinned and gave the top of the car a little pat.

Fulgencio did not know what the name meant, but wishing to be polite, he raised a finger to the brim of his hat. "*Hola, Woodee,*" he said. It's not a Cadillac, he thought, but it has wheels and it will get me home.

The gringo unlocked the door and opened it wide. He reached a hand inside to unlock the back door and swung it open too. "Put your things in there," he said, motioning to the back.

Fulgencio poked his head inside.

The interior was something to behold. It too was covered with wooden panels. And the steering wheel was twice as large as that in most cars. Where the back seat should have been, a narrow mattress was stretched out. On the mattress were piles of clothing, a few pillows minus their cases and a bunched-up serape that was faded and frayed. Beside the mattress, occupying most of the remaining space, sat different-sized cartons spilling over with various objects. There were two nested mountains of straw hats, a boxful of sheathed machetes and stacks of undershirts imprinted with foreign words and colorful designs. There were piles of audiocassettes, small transistor radios and calculators no wider than one's palm. There were pottery platters and vases and jugs. A number of miniature mariachi bands—each group comprised of stuffed, dried frogs wearing fancy little sombreros and playing miniature instruments—sat in a corner of the car.

"*Ay, chihuahua,*" Fulgencio said under his breath. The gringo had a small *mercado* here. Fulgencio wondered how the man had amassed so much merchandise, but he would never pose such an indelicate question. Being in business himself, he knew it was a man's right to protect the secrets of his trade.

Fulgencio picked up his valise and stowed it halfway back on the mattress. He wedged his tripod between the case and the back of the front seat. In no time, he and the gringo were on the road heading for Santiago.

It was not yet dark and the traffic was light. Fulgencio Llanos sat back, his elbow jutting out the open window. He glanced over at the gringo. "Those mariachi bands in back . . .," Fulgencio said.

"*¿Sí?*"

"The frogs. Do you plan to sell them or are you

collecting them?" Fulgencio threw in the last half of the question so as not to appear meddlesome. The truth was he could not imagine why a person would want to collect something as unsightly as dead frogs with hard bulging bellies and matchstick legs.

The gringo kept his eyes on the road. "Are you a buying man, or just a curious one?"

"I'm curious, I guess, because if you plan to sell the frogs, I have a proposition."

"And what is that?" This time the gringo turned his face to Fulgencio.

"I could photograph the frogs. I could set the bands up with interesting backdrops and photograph them. You could buy my photographs and then sell them yourself."

"You think so?"

"Yes, I really think so."

The gringo turned his gaze back up to the road again.

"So, what do you think?" Fulgencio said after giving the gringo a moment or two to mull it over. "I could set little palm trees behind the frog at the marimba. The two with guitars, I could set under a balcony as if they were serenading a señorita. I don't know if there are girl frogs, but I could put a wig on the one with the trumpet." He knew that there were no palm trees, no balcony, no wig among his props, but these were minor details that for now he could ignore.

"I don't think so," the gringo said after a moment. "*¿No?*"

"*No, creo que no.*" The gringo gave a toothy smile.

Fulgencio shrugged and returned the smile. "*Muy bien.*" He was surprised at how readily he himself had backed down. But who could blame him. It was the end of the day and he was tired. Besides, after his trip to the capital next week, people would beg him for any kind of photograph.

Fulgencio turned his attention to the countryside rolling by. Now and then they passed a small roadside shrine that marked the place of a fatal accident. Though there were dangers present in these twisting roads, Fulgencio enjoyed traveling along them by car. He much preferred it to the bus. He pushed his hat back and leaned against the door, squinting into the wind. He liked the feel of the rushing air. He could smell the salty odor of the sea, the subtle fragrance of the lemon groves they passed. Fulgencio glanced over to the gringo who was lighting up a cigarette. Now the odor of tobacco mixed in with all the others.

"*¿Un cigarro?*" The gringo extended a pack of Delicados.

Fulgencio shook his head. "*No, gracias.*" He did not smoke cigarettes or any other kind of tobacco. He knew this was unusual for a man, but with him, that's the way it was. Lupe Bustos admired that about him. "I like to kiss your mouth, Fulgencio Llanos," she had whispered to him one night when they were lying across her bed. "Your mouth tastes very good to me." Thinking of Lupe Bustos, of the sweet taste of *her* mouth, Fulgencio wished that he were driving. If he were behind the wheel, he would step more heavily on the gas pedal. He would cause the car to fly to Lupe Bustos's *comedor.*

A shift in the way the wind struck his face brought Fulgencio out of his reverie. The gringo was slowing down. They were halfway to Santiago, and the gringo was putting on the brakes. "*¿Qué pasa?*" Fulgencio asked.

"That's the road to Playa de Oro," the gringo said. He pointed past Fulgencio to a road that lay just ahead and off to the right. A sign marking the road read PLAYA DE ORO—5 km. When the gringo reached the turnoff, he veered onto the road, the tires squealing in protest. Flung in the gringo's direction, Fulgencio placed a hand on the dashboard to steady himself. He could hear the merchandise slipping and sliding in the back. He glanced quickly behind him to check on his equipment. He could not see his tripod, but his valise looked undisturbed.

"Don't worry," the gringo said, pointing over his shoulder. "Everything is fine back there." He flicked the lighted stub of his cigarette out his opened window. "I want to see the beach," he said, nodding in the direction straight ahead.

"*Ah, la playa.*" Fulgencio managed a weak smile. What else could he do? He reminded himself that accepting a ride put him at the mercy of the driver's whims. Still, this side trip irked him. He had never been to this beach before, but from the sign back there, the drive to it and back should take ten or fifteen minutes. *Paciencia, Fulgencio, paciencia,* he told himself. Laying eyes on Lupe Bustos would have to wait for now.

The road to Playa de Oro was cobblestoned and narrow. It curved sharply around dust-covered trees and dense vegetation. The going was slow because of the curves and because of the sudden washes in the road where cobblestones were missing. The gringo swung the car around the washes. He and Fulgencio bobbed up and down on the seats.

"The road is bad," the gringo said.

"*Sí, muy malo.*" Fulgencio visualized the beer he'd had at the cantina sloshing around inside him. He could hear the boxes in the back bouncing against each other. He threw an arm over the back of the seat, placing a protective hand on the top of his valise.

They had been on the road just a few minutes when night began to show itself. Darkness came down through the trees and settled over them. The gringo pulled a switch and light leaped from the car and penetrated the gloomy outline of the woods slipping past them.

Fulgencio glanced over to see the gringo light up a second cigarette. The glow of the match cast a shadow over the curve of his cheek and up the side of his nose. Fulgencio looked quickly out the window again. Along the side of the road, the trees appeared huge and eerily distorted. A fear as misshapened as the trees came over him. Just who was this man, anyway? Since turning off the main road, he had hardly said a word. It was as if his friendliness had dissolved with the end of daylight. A terrible realization came to him. The gringo was out to rob him. Just as he must have robbed who knows how many shops of all that merchandise in back. It was the camera he wanted, Fulgencio was sure of it. He recalled how the gringo had asked about it. What a fool he'd been to tell him what he had. Fulgencio's mind raced to formulate a plan. He could open the door and jump from the car. He could do it, right now, the car was going slow enough. But if he did, he would have to leave his camera behind. The photographs of El Santo. He could never do that. He would wait until they reached the beach. He remembered the machetes in the back. If worst came to worst, he would reach for a machete.

From over the trees came the faraway sound of vesper bells and to Fulgencio, the tolling was like the voice of God calling out to him. He was not a churchgoing man, but he was a God-fearing one, and so he struck a bargain with the Lord. Señor, he thought, if You withdraw this danger, I will be a better man. He made a quick list of personal improvements. He would not take paper wreaths from road shrines to liven up his sittings. Because times were bad, he would decrease by a few hundred pesos his markup on the sizing and the framing. He would be more honest, less overly complimentary of the way that people looked, of their bleak possessions. He would do this even if it meant foregoing a few sales.

Fulgencio cut short his litany. Up ahead, the road widened and there was the sound of the surf. The air grew heavier, more humid. Leaving the road and trees behind, the car emerged under a dark canopy of sky. The gringo turned onto the beach. He pulled to a stop in the sand.

The headlights fanned out over a wild sea that crashed a slate-colored surf against the beach and the rocks clustered at one end of it. For a moment, the sight of the sea transported Fulgencio, but then he came quickly to his senses. He scanned the shoreline for signs of others, realizing in a rush that, just as the road had been deserted, so was the beach.

"The beach is good," the gringo said. He took a last pull from his cigarette and tossed it out the window.

Fulgencio was heartened by the gringo's voice, by the renewed friendliness in it, but he was wary just the same.

"What is that?" The gringo stuck his arm out the window and pointed.

Looking up the beach, Fulgencio saw what looked like a mountain rising from the sand.

"*Vamos*," the gringo said. He put the car in gear, and they went bumping off over the sand.

Fulgencio steadied himself against the back of the seat. Just what was that over there? As they drew near, he saw it was a building. A dark, abandoned building.

The gringo pulled up to it and stopped. He turned off the motor. "It looks like a hotel," he said.

The man was right. Caught in the glare of the headlights was the shell of an unfinished hotel. Empty door frames and window frames looked out across the beach. The gringo opened his door, lighting up the car's interior, and got out. A moment later, he returned and poked his head in the car. "Want to come?"

A movie Fulgencio'd once seen popped into his head. It was about a crazy gringo who took his family to a deserted hotel in the mountains. In the mountains, he went after his family with an ax. Fulgencio's scalp prickled at the remembrance of the man's face, of the insane look in his eyes, of the high-pitched way that he had laughed. Despite these thoughts, Fulgencio managed a friendly little wave. "*Andale*," he said to the gringo. "I'll wait here." Until he could be sure of the man's next move, he would stay in the car with the machetes.

"*Bien.*" The gringo slammed the door shut and the inside of the car went dark again.

Fulgencio kept his eye on the gringo. The sheen of the headlights struck the gringo's back, throwing a giant shadow against the building. Soon both shadow and man disappeared through one of the yawning doorways.

Left behind, Fulgencio developed a fresh edge to his fear. His heart hammered in his chest. The gringo could be anywhere. He could be slipping out the other side of the building; he could be taking a wide path around the car. Right now he might be creeping up behind him. Lord, Fulgencio thought, please help me now, and to show the direness of his need, he reached into his heart and handed over to the Lord the one gift he was certain would extricate him from this danger. From this day forward, he pledged, I'll attend Mass every Sunday. He would sit in the front pew so the Lord could best see him. He would pronounce the Mass's responses in a sonorous voice and so give witness to the miracle of his deliverance.

Fulgencio scooted across the seat. He would start up the car. Yes! He would do it. He would drive off and leave the gringo at the beach. Fulgencio groped for the keys, feeling hastily up and down the steering column. There were no keys in the ignition. He leaned into the wheel, running his hand clumsily over the dashboard. No keys there. Fulgencio brought his fist down hard against the wheel. "*¡Chinga!*" He looked out the window. It was time to arm himself. He slid out from behind the steering wheel, turned, and reached back so that he lay halfway into the back of the station wagon.

He had a grip on the hilt of one of the machetes when the inside of the car lighted up. Fulgencio gasped as the gringo scrambled in. For an instant, it was as if Fulgencio's heart had stopped.

"*Mis machetes,*" the gringo said, his voice high and tremulous.

Fulgencio let go of the machete. He drew himself slowly back down on the seat.

"*¿Qué pasa aquí?*" the gringo said, a twitch pulling at the corner of his eye. His hat sat crookedly on the back of his head. His face appeared enormous and grotesque under the dome light.

"*Nada, Señor, nada.*" For proof, Fulgencio turned his hands up.

In a surprisingly quick move, the gringo reached across Fulgencio, pinning him for a moment against the back of the seat. The gringo tugged at the handle and thrust the door open. "*¡Fuera!*" he exclaimed.

The surf roared in Fulgencio's ears and he was stunned into immobility.

"I said get out. Get out now!"

One moment Fulgencio was in the car and now he lay half sprawled on the beach of Playa de Oro. He scrambled up, losing his footing for a moment in the loose sand. "But, Señor," he yelled, "you do not understand." He struggled to his feet again and was reaching for the door, when the car started up. Its wheels spun and its back end fishtailed before it pulled away.

"*¡Señor! ¡Señor!*" Fulgencio called, racing as fast as

the sand allowed. He waved his arms wildly.

Ahead, the car cast two beams of milky light out toward the road and the trees lining it. Fulgencio trained his eyes on the light, a beacon, his heart pounding louder now than even the surf. "Wait," he yelled, running on a few more meters before he saw that catching up would be impossible.

The gringo's lights floated out over the beach and then over the road before they were swallowed up in the trees. *Madre de Dios,* Fulgencio thought. He sank to his knees as the darkness fell over him.

Fulgencio Llanos looked up into the vastness stretching above him. A few stars twinkled now, and their cheeriness mocked him. Please Lord, he muttered, but he stopped there, for he could not think of the good in his life so that he might offer it up for bargaining. He dug his hands into the sand, feeling the cool moistness between his fingers and under him where he sat. He was alone. It was now only himself and the deafening sea. He had no camera. No equipment. No photographs of El Santo to turn his life in a new direction.

Standing, Fulgencio allowed his eyes to adjust to the darkness. The surf pounded around him as if he were trapped inside a drum. He looked out across the beach, to the road that led away from here. It would take an hour, he figured to reach the highway. He emptied his shoes of sand and started out, the awareness of what he lacked was a sharpness in his chest. He felt light without his possessions, unsubstantial and unimportant, as if he might float away without his valise to anchor him. He came to the place where the beach left off and the cobbled road began, and he emptied his shoes of sand again before continuing. It was darker on the road, and at each side of him the trees and brush offered large conspiring shadows.

He had walked perhaps a minute or two when he came around a bend. He stopped short.

Someone was crouched by the roadside.

"¿*Quién es?*" he called, fearful it was the gringo waiting to spring on him. But no response came, and the object did not move when he clapped his hands on the chance it was some animal that had scurried out from the brush.

Fulgencio approached the object cautiously. When he neared it, he could not believe his eyes.

It was his valise.

He dropped down upon it, throwing his arms around it as if he'd found a lost child. He opened the valise, and in the light of the moon that just now showed itself, he saw the bulky outline of his camera. He groped around inside and felt the plates of film containing his bright new future. He gave a whoop and it was then he saw his tripod, lying in the road up ahead. Fulgencio closed his valise and hurried over to his tripod and scooped it up. He raised it high above his head and broke into a little dance. In spite of the cobbles in the road, he leaped and dipped and hollered and, after a moment, laid his tripod across his valise and sank down beside the two.

Fulgencio Llanos sat there for a time, his hand resting on all he needed to be somebody. He shook off the chill he felt at the thought of what might have been. He tried to make sense of his puzzling predicament. Why had the gringo dropped off his equipment? Hadn't the man wanted to rob him? Two images clicked in place in Fulgencio's mind: his own hand on the hilt of the machete and the look on the gringo's face when he'd returned to the car.

Fulgencio hung his head as understanding washed over him. What a crazy thing, Fulgencio thought. I feared the gringo and the gringo feared me. Tucking the tripod under an arm, he picked up his valise, its weight a comfort. He'd gone just a few paces when he stepped on his hat.

Fulgencio Llanos threw back his head and gave a laugh. "Hombre, Fulgencio," he said, "you've been a fool." He plucked up his hat and plopped it on his head, starting toward the highway again. He was hungry for a plate of shrimp and Lupe's salsa for dipping. On Sunday, he decided, he'd take Lupe on an outing. He would wait outside the church for her and then they would head for the beach. Taking her hand, they would run into the waves until the sea cradled them.

Yes, he thought, come Sunday, he would celebrate.

Chapter 5

Marta Rodríguez

La Recamarera
(recamarera, n.f. chambermaid)

Marta Rodríguez pushed the cleaning cart down the winding hallway of the hotel. Bottles of cleaner held in tubs attached to the side of the cart struck each other, tinkling as she went. Marta reached to silence the bottles. She laid a hand over her belly as if with an open palm she might keep her pregnancy from view. Her condition was humiliating. Already her uniform was tight around the middle. Marta came to the end of the hall and knocked loudly on the door of the round-arched entrance to number eight. When there was no answer, she used the passkey to let herself in.

The room was in disorder. The bed was a jumble of linens. Beyond the bathroom door, she spotted towels heaped on the floor. Here, in the bedroom, clothing was flung over chairs. Dirty ashtrays and used tissues were scattered on the dresser. Food-spotted plates and empty glasses were stacked on a serving tray. Marta sighed. This was her last room, and she had hoped to breeze through it. She was eager to be out of the hotel and at her sister's house. Today, Chayo was making paper flowers and Marta was happy to be able to help. It was the least that she could do. Chayo and Cande were taking the baby. Once the baby was in Chayo's hands, Marta would be free.

Marta closed the door halfway. She hurried to the stack of magazines she spied on the bedside table. Of all the things that tourists traveled with, it was American magazines that intrigued her the most. Their glossy pages presented an orderly world, perfectly captured. A world that she was determined to soon experience.

Marta picked up a magazine off the top of the stack. "*Ay, Leefay, mi favorita,*" she said. Though she was rushed, she would take a quick look before getting down to work. This issue of *Life* featured Elizabeth Taylor on the cover. Marta loved Elizabeth Taylor. She loved her thick lashes, the smudge of violet on her eyelids. Marta opened the magazine and paged through the pictures. She allowed the pictures to conjure up the dream that for months she had sheltered in her heart. She had not voiced the dream aloud for fear that sharing it would dispel its promise.

Her dream was this: Once the baby was born, once she had turned it over to Chayo, Marta would leave Santiago. She would head north, across the border, to El Paso. In El Paso there would be work in a house as cool and dazzling white as the hotel. In the house she would have a room just to herself, a room like the one she now came upon in the magazine. It had a thick carpet and a bed crowned at the head with a golden sunburst of brass. Next to the bed there was an easy chair at arm's length from a television set. Marta Rodríguez ran her hand over the smooth, lustrous page. She saw herself in the room, relaxing in the chair. She saw herself rising to answer a knock on the door. She saw the lady of the house standing at the door. I don't know what I would do without you,

Marta, the lady said. She smiled, laying in Marta's palm a series of crisp green bills that were of far more value than the limp drab ones of Mexico.

Closing the magazine, Marta laid it down upon the others. At the window she looked out on the sea and the series of whitecaps racing each other to the shore. She thought of Roberto Ramos, who had hastily left town. Try as she might, she could not forget that night on the beach. The sound of the surf was in her ears when she had allowed him a kiss and then another. He had started to lay her down. She had given a little laugh, thinking she could stop him. She had found that she was wrong.

Marta walked over to the bed. She jerked the linens from the mattress and piled them on the floor. She snatched up one of the pillows, peeled off the case and flung it on the sheets.

"¡Hola!" a voice called out. Luz Gamboa was at the door. She came into the room, her pink thongs slapping against the floor tiles. Luz's hair was piled in a tangle atop her head. Her eyelids were a smoldering blue, eye shadow that no doubt she'd found among some tourist's cosmetics. Luz looked around. "This room's a mess."

"I just started in here," Marta said. The child rolled inside her, and she paused for a moment before wrenching the last pillow from its case.

Luz stood in the middle of the room, her hands on her hips. "Well," she said, "someone I know is not very happy."

Marta threw the pillowcase next to the others. "Help me with the linens," she said, and they went out into the hall and Marta squatted beside the cart. She picked out sheets and towels from the bottom shelf, but before she could stand with them, the child kicked sharply and she lost her balance and had to catch herself. "¡Híjole!" Luz said, rushing over from around the cart. "*¿Estás bien?*"

"*Sí, sí. Toma,*" Marta said, handing the linens to her friend. It was embarrassing to be so clumsy. She had to use the side of the cart to pull herself up. Would she ever be herself again?

The two went back into the room, and Luz, her arms full, nudged the door shut with a thrust of her hip. She dumped the linens on the chair next to the window. "I can't stay," Luz said. She went to the dresser and tipped the edge of the tray up and looked under it before setting it down again. "I'm on my last room. All that was safe to take all day was a few hundred pesos." Luz was stealing bits of money from tourists because she had two young children to raise alone now that her man, Tito, had run off to El Paso with Tula Fuentes. Luz said a woman never loves a man as much as when he leaves her, and so to get Tito back, she had turned to Remedios. To reawaken Tito's ardor for his wife, *la curandera* had rinsed two of the couple's handkerchiefs in *el agua del desencanto.*

Though she had not said so, Marta did not approve of her friend's stealing. If she kept it up and was caught, Luz would be fired. As for Remedios, Marta was curious about *la curandera,* and about her water of disenchantment. Marta did not truly believe, though, that the healer's washes would bring Tito back.

Luz went over to the bedside table and moved aside the magazines to see if there might be money under them.

"Leave those things alone," Marta said. "This is my room to clean and I don't want you looking here."

"All right, all right," Luz said, poking her fingers into her hair.

Marta unfurled a sheet over the bed as if it were a net she was casting into the sea. The sheet was bleached white. The fresh smell of the mangle was released into the room.

"Remedios is doing another wash for me," Luz said.

"How many has she done?"

Luz waved a hand in the air. "What does it matter how many she's done. The important thing is that she does them. Tito needs help. You remember how it was. You remember how Tula Fuentes came home from El Paso. You remember how she strutted through town, how she pranced and swayed to catch Tito's eye." Luz began to pace, her arms crossed over her breasts, her expression dark and furious. "Tula Fuentes had a spell put on my man. She went to *el brujo* and paid him to do it. She and the sorcerer whipped my man into a frenzy. Tito had no choice but to fall for Tula's charms."

Marta felt sorry to have urged Luz into such a painful remembrance. She went to her friend and put an arm around her and gave her a squeeze. "It's all right. It will happen like you say. Before you know it, Remedios's *agua del desencanto* will put an end to *el brujo*'s spell." It was really a matter of good over bad, and wasn't good always the victor? Frequently, Marta had passed *el brujo*'s place on the road to Manzanillo. The sorcerer's house was painted as purple as an eggplant. It sat pushed back from the highway, ringed by a wall of organ cactus. At night an unnatural light drifted from the house and it struck the cacti, casting shadows slender as horses' shanks, across the road. Just the thought of it now unnerved Marta. She drew up her shoulders to shake off the feeling.

Luz gave a little wave and smiled so that the silvery cap on her front tooth showed plainly. "Well," she said, "I have to go. After work, I'll walk home with you."

Marta shook her head. "Not today. I'm going to Chayo's. Today I'm helping with the flowers."

Later, after she'd finished the room and changed

out of her uniform, Marta Rodríguez walked down the dry riverbed that cut through Santiago before ending a stone's throw from the sea. It was after four and still hot. A foulness drifted up from the puddles of stagnant water pooling in the arroyo. Marta skirted one of the puddles. She shooed away a rusty-colored hen that was in her path. It scampered up the slope and joined a clutch of other chickens foraging in the yard of one of the dwellings bordering the riverbed. Bersa, *la tortillera,* emerged from a house and tossed a panful of water at the chickens. They squawked and rose in a feathery flurry and scurried off around the house. Bersa tucked the pan under an arm and looked Marta's way before disappearing inside. She did not wave as Marta hoped she might. It wasn't surprising; in Santiago she was the talk of town. Marta kicked at a pebble and sent it flying. She saw herself four months from now, boarding the bus to El Paso. In El Paso she would start over.

When Marta reached Chayo's house, her sister was sitting out under the lime tree. Marta flung the string bag she carried over her shoulder and went up the slope. She walked over to her sister. Squares of crepe paper in scarlet, ocher and saffron were stacked beside Chayo's stool. "You're working outside today," Marta said.

"It's so hot." Chayo pressed the back of a hand to her forehead. Her fingers were tinted dark from working with so many colors. "You're lucky to spend your day in a cool place." She was making hibiscus flowers, and now she inserted a dark stamen sprouting tiny yellow pistils into the throat of a scarlet blossom.

Marta looked over Chayo's shoulder at the blue door of the house. "Is Cande home?" Since losing his restaurant job some months before, Candelario had not found work. For some weeks, he had been fishing and selling his catch at the stands in the market. To make a little extra, he rode the bucking bulls in the town's Sunday rodeo when he was lucky enough to get a turn.

Chayo laid the blossom she was making in her lap. "He went out very early."

"How's the fishing? Has it been good?"

"No. It's as if no fish lived in the sea."

Marta observed the sudden slump of her sister's shoulders. She noted the way Chayo's stained fingers cupped the lushness of the blossom resting in her lap. "Maybe I can help," Marta said. "I can give you a little money." She said this though her pay was already thinly divided. There was the rent for the room she and tía Fina occupied, the meals to be bought for them both. There was the fee for periodic visits to the midwife, as well as saving for the upcoming cost of the child's delivery.

But there was one more thing that separated Marta from her money. Each week, after seeing to all the rest, she poked ten thousand pesos into the pottery jar hidden under her bed. Already there was one hundred thousand pesos in the jar, money she would use to make her getaway.

"You have money?" Chayo said.

Looking down, Marta leaned against the lime tree. She picked at the side of her thumbnail. "I've been saving." When she said this, she did not raise her face to her sister, lest Chayo see reflected in her eyes the white house in El Paso with the room and the television and the chair. "Esperanza Clemente has to be paid," she added. "The midwife doesn't deliver babies for free, you know."

"Tita," Chayo said, her voice trailing off. She stood up, laying the blossom she was making on the ground beside her.

Marta looked up. It wasn't every day that Chayo used her nickname.

"*¿Qué te pasa?*"

"We can't take your baby," Chayo said.

Marta stepped away from the lime tree. She stepped back from her sister, who was coming toward her, her doe eyes wide and glistening.

"What are you saying?" Marta said.

"Cande and I. We're having a baby of our own."

Marta laughed. The news was absurd. "You can't have babies."

"It's true. I've been to the midwife. We can't take your baby, Tita. Cande says we can't."

Chayo reached out a hand, but Marta moved away from it. "Cande said you'd take my baby. Remember when he said it? We were sitting under this lime tree when he said it." As if it might bear witness, Marta pointed feebly to the tree.

"I know he said it. But now we can't. Things have changed and now we can't."

Marta Rodríguez cried out. It was a short, plaintive cry. Her face burned as though there were nettles under her skin. She turned and stumbled down the arroyo's slope. As she ran, she heard her sister calling out to her.

* * *

Marta was out of breath when she reached the rooming house. The *mesón* had twelve one-room apartments set around a large treeless patio. Marta's room was directly across the patio from Luz's. Marta hurried there now.

"Thank God you're home," Marta said, leaning up against Luz's door. Luz was at the dresser, pulling a brush through her hair.

"Something happened." Marta went in and collapsed on the bed. The room seemed to spin, and she closed her eyes against the feel of it.

"*¿Qué pasó? ¿Qué fue?*"

Marta opened her eyes to see Luz bending over her.

Luz's hair was a wild halo around her face.

"Chayo is pregnant. She says she and Cande won't take my baby."

"Chayo? Pregnant?"

"The midwife says she is."

Luz sat on the edge of the bed. She smoothed her hair back from her face. "Well, then, that makes it so. Esperanza Clemente doesn't make mistakes."

"I know." Marta pulled herself up to sit next to Luz. After a moment, Luz spoke up. "You know, raising a baby is not the worst thing. Look at me. I have two to raise. All mothers do it. You can do it, too."

"You don't understand." Marta bunched her hands into her lap. The truth was that Luz was older. She was twenty-two, while Marta was only sixteen. Marta had a dream, and there was no room for a baby in that dream.

"I know how you feel now, but after the baby comes, it will all be different." The tone in Luz's voice was clearly meant to soothe. She rubbed little circles over Marta's back. "When the baby comes, you will love it. After you've held the little thing, you won't want it out of your sight. Just wait. You'll see."

"I hate Cande," Marta said, picking at the geometric designs sprinkled on her dress. "If he wanted to, he and Chayo could still take my baby. Just because they're having one, that shouldn't mean they can't take mine. I'd help them with money. I'd give them part of my salary. It's not like I wouldn't. That part was all arranged. Look at your sister, you pay her and she keeps your two."

"Yes, but she only keeps them while I work. What you want is different. You want someone to raise your child. That is very different."

Marta turned her face to Luz. "Given my circumstances, can you blame me?"

Marcela, Luz's daughter, ran in. She was four years old. She was a slender girl with large, dark eyes that were slightly crossed. "My brother is a monster," she said, stamping a small sandaled foot. "He says I am ugly." Marcela's chin crumpled and she began to cry.

Luz went to the door. "¡José Mario!" she yelled out into the patio. José Mario was six and Marta could see him peeking out from around the toilet shack. He popped out of view when his mother called out. Marcela ran over to Luz and buried her face in her mother's skirt. "Sometimes I just don't know," Luz said. She patted her daughter's head.

Marta left the bed and mumbled good-bye. She crossed the patio and went into her room. The television was blaring. The set, resting on a dresser, was a small black-and-white with two antennae clumped with tinfoil and spread wide. The picture was snowy. Periodically, it rolled up toward the top of the screen. Tía Fina sat in her chair, watching it, her legs propped on a stool. "*Mira, es Juan Travolta,*" she said.

Marta glanced at the television. The movie *Vaselina* was playing. John Travolta's hair was slicked back, and the way he swaggered across the screen reminded her of Roberto Ramos. Marta fell onto the bed. She stared up at the ceiling. A song drifted out from the television and it stirred something in her that spoke of El Paso and the promise waiting for her up north, across the border. Marta tucked her legs up and tried to pull herself into a ball, but the baby kept her from it. She began to cry then, softly, so tía Fina would not notice. She laid her fists against her temples. She had allowed herself only nine months with the child, and now the child would fill her years. In the future, there would be no days without the child.

Beyond the opened door of the room, a commotion rose up. Marta wiped her eyes. She propped herself up on an elbow.

"Someone's yelling," tía Fina said. She craned her neck in the direction of the door. "Go take a look."

Marta sighed and got up, sure it was the children playing in the patio. She went to the door and looked out.

It was Luz's daughter who was yelling. Marcela and her brother were in front of their door. Marcela jumped up and down. José Mario stood still as a stone next to her. Luz was there too, her hands raised halfway to her face.

It was a man who captured their attention. Though his back was to Marta, she did not have to guess at who he was.

"Tito," Marta said, stepping back into the room.

"What is it?" tía Fina said.

"It's Tito Gamboa," Marta said, switching off the television. "He's come back to Luz." Marta poked her head outside again. Luz's door was closed now and her family was no longer in sight. Old don Justo, Marta's next-door neighbor, had come out onto the gallery. Yoyo, his German shepherd, had come out too. Don Justo waved at Marta when he saw her. "Tito's back," he said, pointing across the patio. Marta walked over. Don Justo was *un pajarero*, a birdman. He had a cageful of canaries, and each day he worked the beach. For a fee, the birds performed tricks for tourists. As a finale, one of the birds plucked up with its beak little printed fortunes from a box filled with them. Since Tito had run off, Luz was a faithful customer. Don Justo's fortunes, she said, gave her answers to life's riddles. "Do you think your fortunes predicted this?" Marta asked. Yoyo was sitting in a shaft of weakening sun. She scratched the dog's head.

Don Justo shrugged. "*¿Quién sabe?* Maybe so."

Marta gave a laugh. "Maybe so." From time to time, for a lark, she had bought fortunes for herself.

She still remembered one of them. It contained an "astral message" cautioning her to be on guard against flatterers whose secret aim was deception. The warning was clear, but it had come too late. There had been no greater flatterer than Roberto Ramos.

"Your aunt is calling," don Justo said.

"Oh," Marta said, "I have to go."

"Where were you?" tía Fina asked. "One minute you're here and the next you disappear."

"I was talking to Don Justo."

"Well," she said. And then, "It's Luz's bad luck Tito's returned." Tía Fina shook her head. "I wouldn't want a man who'd been off with someone else. Would you want that?"

"I don't want a man, period," Marta said. She thought of don Justo's fortunes. She thought of Remedios's *agua del desencanto* and how it had brought Tito home again. Had she not seen him herself, she wouldn't have believed it.

Marta steadied herself against the dresser because the child gave a little kick at the same time a thought struck her that was like a kick inside her head. There were unseen powers in the world and if she began to trust them like Luz clearly did, maybe her problems would be remedied. Remedios, she thought. She would go to Remedios. What had worked for Luz could work for her. *La curandera* and her potions would prompt Cande's change of heart.

* * *

The next day, after work, Marta Rodríguez was in Remedios's hut. It was her first time here. The hut was simply furnished. There was a cot, a dresser in one corner, a table and chairs in another. Grasses and herbs hung in bunches from the ceiling. A second table was near a window but Marta did not allow her eyes to rest too long on it. There were lighted candles on the table, some white, some black. There was incense burning and it threw up a spiral of smoke and an acrid stench. There were objects on the table, the sight of which was unsettling. Marta followed *la curandera* to the empty table. The healer was old. She had a face like the bark of some ancient tree. Tall and big boned, her body appeared more youthful than her face. A long skinny braid was draped like an inverted question mark down her back. When Remedios pulled one of the chairs out from under the table, a striped cat napping on the seat gave a sharp meow and jumped off. Marta stepped back. Cats frightened her. In the *mesón* she'd heard tell of a cat smothering a baby while it slept in its hammock. Another cat, a black one, awakened perhaps by the yowl of the first, crept out from under the table. Both cats leaped through one of the hut's opened windows.

Remedios seemed not to notice the cats nor Marta's uneasiness. She motioned for Marta to sit. "So Luz Gamboa is a friend of yours," Remedios said.

Marta nodded.

When they were both seated, Remedios said, "Let's not waste each other's time. *Dame las manos.*"

Marta laid her hands in Remedios's and the old one closed her eyes. Her hands were very hot and she clasped Marta's gently, swaying a little as she did. Soon a deep vibrating hum came from somewhere deep within her, and after a moment Remedios opened her eyes. "This condition of yours," she said, jutting her chin in the direction of Marta's belly. "It happened against your will."

"*Es cierto,*" Marta said, feeling tears welling up. In all this time hardly anyone had believed her. She had spoken the truth to her family. She had told them about the beach, about the sting the sea grass had made against her thighs and buttocks. She had told them about Roberto's suffocating weight, about his hand pressed hard over her mouth. She said all this and more, but her family had not believed the way it truly happened. She could tell it in their eyes, in the fact that her story had not raised their indignation.

Marta did not withdraw her hands from the warmth of Remedios's grasp. "I need your help," Marta said, then she went on, allowing all her story to spill out.

"I see," Remedios said after Marta had grown silent.

"Can you make Cande change his mind? Can you use one of your potions to make him do it? I can pay. I work at the hotel, so I can pay."

"Child, this is not a question of money or of potions."

"What do you mean?" If not these things, what then?

"I will say this as gently as I can." The healer's large hooded eyes softened in the way a person's do when preparing another for bad news. Marta pulled her hands away from the healer's and dropped them into her lap.

"A girl like you," Remedios said, "a girl like you should not go across the border."

Remedios's pronouncement was a blow. "But you don't understand . . ."

"*Un momento*," Remedios said, holding up a hand. "*El norte* is a place where girls like you are lost. It is a place that hardens and ruins girls like you."

"I am ruined already," Marta Rodríguez said, passing a hand over her belly. She felt her heart hardening against this old woman who talked as if she knew her.

"You are not ruined. True, you've had your share of troubles, but going north would only give you more."

Marta pushed back her chair and stood. "I came because I want you to make Cande change his mind. Will you do it or not?"

"I can do it, but I will not." Remedios pushed back her own chair, but she did not rise. "You must listen to me when I tell you that I see things about you that you do not know about yourself."

For some moments Marta was silent, the dream of her getaway swirling like a wild wind inside her. "And so you won't help me," she said at length.

"I will not help you if it means helping you reach *el norte*."

"With your help or not, I'm going there."

"Very well," Remedios said, standing now and heading for the door. "There is nothing more to say."

"No, there is nothing more to say."

Marta left the hut as the orange ball of sun slipped below the tops of the trees in Remedios's yard. In the distance, the sea was a dark pane of glass and Marta thought that her life seemed as bleak as this sea. El Paso, she said to herself. I *will* go to El Paso. She repeated the words in a cadence that propelled her down the hill and along the road that led into Santiago. With each step she felt more determined and sure of herself. She did not need Remedios and her silly potions. Marta herself would go to Cande. She would explain the problem and Cande would listen. In the end, because they were family, Cande would change his mind.

It was Candelario himself who opened the door. He and Chayo were eating, and Chayo jumped up from the table when Marta came in. "Tita," Chayo said, rushing over. "Yesterday you left so quickly."

"Here I am," Marta said.

"Come and eat," Chayo said, hurrying back to the table. She pushed a plate in her sister's direction.

"I'm not hungry." Marta dropped into a chair. Candelario had gone back to eating, his head inclined over his plate.

Chayo moved a fork through the mound of beans

on her plate. "Yesterday, after you left, I thought you were too angry to come back."

"I'm not angry. I'm happy about your baby. I didn't say it yesterday, but I am." She touched Candelario's shoulder. "I'm happy for you too, Cande."

Candelario looked up and smiled at her and then continued eating.

Candelario's smile was like a signal to Marta. "Do you think when my baby comes, you and Chayo can still take it? I know you told Chayo that you couldn't, but do you think you could change your mind? I am going to El Paso. I'll have work there. If it's money you need, I'll send you everything I make."

Candelario put his fork down. "I didn't tell Chayo we couldn't take your baby. I promised to take it, and once I give my word, that is that."

"But Chayo said . . ."

"It's your sister who does not want it now. It's Chayo who changed her mind."

Marta gasped. She turned to look at Chayo, who was coming around the table.

"It's not what you think," Chayo said. "It's just that when my baby comes, I want it to be only Cande and the baby and me." She dropped down beside Marta's chair as if she were asking for a blessing. "This is my first baby, Tita. I have waited a long time for it."

Marta's chair scraped across the floor. "You lied to me," she said. "My only sister lied to me." She turned and, for the second time in as many days, fled from her sister's house.

Outside it was growing dark. Marta went down the arroyo until she was in town. She walked aimlessly down one street and then another, her mind numb to the presence of others and to the shadows that had begun to fill the doorways of the houses along the way. Soon she came to the highway at the edge of town. She stopped and looked across it. *El brujo's* house stood there, and Marta nodded as if to acknowledge the way fate had placed her here. She crossed the highway and walked into the yard.

El brujo, don Picho Lara, emerged from a wide ravine that started a few meters from the back of his house. A large black dog was at his side and it spotted Marta first. The dog barked and rushed up to Marta who held herself rigid and tried to look fearless. "Don Picho," she cried, "call the dog back."

El brujo clapped sharply. "¡Diablo!" he yelled and the dog trotted back to him.

An eye out for the dog, Marta went toward the sorcerer, who was short and thick and powerful in appearance. He wore loose-fitting trousers, and a blousy shirt. Serpents and jaguars were embroidered on the shirt. "*¿Quién sos?*" he asked.

"Marta Rodríguez."

"*¿A qué venís?*"

Why had she come? Because she had a sister who would not honor a family member's right to ask a favor of another. "It's my sister. She is very selfish."

El brujo pointed to a pair of chairs sitting under a span of corrugated tin jutting from the roof. The two went over and sat down. The dog sprawled between them. "So, tell me more."

Marta Rodríguez plunged into her story, and the sorcerer studied her while she spoke, his fingers stroking the goatee sprouting from his chin. "Do you think you can do something?" Marta asked when she was finished.

El brujo gave a devilish smile. "Oh, there's plenty I can do."

"There is?" she said, wondering to herself why this surprised her.

"There is."

Marta rearranged herself in the chair. "And the cost?"

El brujo fingered what looked like a rabbit's foot hanging from a cord draped around his neck. "*Todo depende,*" he said.

"I need a price," she said, emboldened by the thought of the coil of bills concealed in the jar under her bed.

He waved his hand as though in irritation. "Very well, the price is ten thousand pesos."

"And what will you do for the money?"

It had grown much darker. *El brujo*'s face was now in shadow, and the serpents and jaguars on his shirt were indistinguishable from one another. "I will cause the child to no longer be a burden."

Marta gave a jump. When she had first learned of her pregnancy, she'd been determined to see a certain doctor who could wipe clean the slate of her encumbered life. But now . . .

El brujo went on, "I will need something that has been close to the child. Some object of clothing that is worn over the belly. When you bring me this, I can begin."

"But it's too late for me," Marta Rodríguez said. "In four months my baby will come."

At this statement, *el brujo* threw back his head and he laughed so raucously that the dog stood up and looked around. *El brujo* leaned forward so that his rabbit's foot swung away from his neck and dangled in midair. "Girl," he said, "it's not your baby I'm speaking of. It's your sister's. It's her child I'll work my magic on."

Marta felt the blood rush from her face. She pictured *el brujo*'s magic wresting the baby from her sister's womb, but then she pictured her own child taking its place in Chayo's arms.

"What will it be?" the sorcerer asked. "Yes or no?"

Marta Rodríguez's cheeks were hot, and her mouth

was so dry that she felt unable to speak, but she did.

"*Sí,*" she said, surprised only by how right her answer sounded.

Chapter 6

Remedios Elementales: Fuego

(fuego, n.m. fire)

Abuelo Sol is up in the east, bathing Remedios in his soft radiance. Grandfather Sun is the Source of All Things and each morning Remedios faces in his direction as he rises to bless her. She is wrapped, head and shoulders, in a black rebozo, and she crouches next to the cooking hearth that dominates the lean-to attached to the hut. On the ground beside her, the cats have tucked themselves into two bundles at the edge of her skirt. A short time before, she lighted a fire under the *comal*, and soon she will slap tortillas on for breakfast. The fire is hot and bright; it chases away the dank chill of morning.

Remedios swallows up the sun. She pictures her own inner sun glowing as rosily as Abuelo. Fixing on Abuelo's image, Remedios closes her eyes. She hums and sways a little. *Soy fuego*, she murmurs. *Soy luz*. I am light. *Soy alma, soy espíritu*. Each day she affirms herself in this way.

Bathed in the light of the sun, she retells herself a familiar story: Far, very far from here, there grows a tree. Circling the tree are jaguar, coyote, scorpion and lizard. Sitting at the very top of the tree is serpent, huge and fat. Atop serpent's head is a little cage. In the little cage there is a bird.

As she always does when she recounts, Remedios visualizes the tree, it is *un amate*. She pictures the animals and reptiles. The cage, it is fashioned of cane reeds. She envisions the bird captured in the cage. The bird is magpie, *urraca*. It is very black and the tips of its wings are an iridescent green. Its eyes are dark lustrous seeds. Trapped in the cage, it opens its powerful beak and calls out an *urra, urra*.

At its cry, Remedios's spirit rises and covers the distance to the tree, soaring above the creatures. Because a spirit is as light as a sunbeam, it hovers alongside the cage and unhooks the latch. In this way the bird is freed. Urra, urra, *Urraca* calls in gratitude. It tells Remedios, I am your own familiar spirit.

Remedios opens her eyes to a magpie perched on a bottom branch of the *nogal*. It cocks its head and looks her way. She shucks a few grains from an ear of corn lying next to the *comal*. She goes to the tree and offers the corn up. *Urraca* flutters down and gently plucks the gift from Remedios's opened palm. She watches the bird fly off, a grain of *maíz* caught like a tiny sun in its beak.

Chapter 7

Rafael Beltrán

El Maestro
(maestro, n.m. teacher)

Rafael Beltrán watched his students file out the door and into the hall filling up with small children and their rowdy chatter. He gathered books and papers from the desk and placed them in the satchel his mother had given him on the day he started teaching. Over the sixteen years he'd owned it, the satchel had darkened to the color of coffee. The leather was very supple. Rafael wished he could say he was as flexible. Lately he'd been thinking a great deal about his life, and he had come to the conclusion that, at forty-one, he was a stiff and formal man who had allowed life to pass him by.

Satchel in hand, Rafael took his hat from the shelf near the door. He ran a hand over his head. He was losing his hair. Just this morning he'd awakened to more lost strands on his pillow. When shaving, he looked long and hard at himself in the mirror. His face was getting pudgy. His hazel eyes had lost their luster.

Mario Suarez, who also taught the second grade, poked his head into the room. "Some of us are having lunch across the street, at the hotel. You can come if you want."

"I can't," Rafael said with a shake of the head. "But thanks just the same." He put on his hat. "I have papers to correct," he added, patting his satchel as if this would prove it.

"Very well," Mario said. "But you are much too dedicated, my friend. Much too dedicated."

Rafael smiled weakly and shrugged. He watched the teacher go down the hall. Soon he himself went out into the street that was congested with cars and with people on their way to lunch or home for the midday siesta. Stores up and down the block were closing up for the two hottest hours of the day. He headed for the plaza to catch the bus to Santiago, the town where he lived. Going past the hotel, he glimpsed Mario and three other teachers through the restaurant window. Sometimes, on nights he could not sleep, Rafael pictured himself enjoying lunch with his friends. He pictured himself free of the obligation that, each day, sent him home at noon.

At the bus stop, Rafael joined others waiting there. Cuco, the fruit vendor, was at his cart piled with mangoes, papayas, pineapples and limes. The words LA COCHTECA were emblazoned in yellow paint on the front of the cart. Rafael knew them to be Toltec for The Poppy.

"*Buenas tardes, Maestro,*" Cuco said when Rafael came up. "How about a little fruit. I can slice some up for you." He stood under a huge red umbrella attached to the side of the cart.

"Not today, Cuco. We have some left from yesterday."

"How about a story then? I have one called The Midget of Uxmal."

Playfully, Rafael shook a finger at Cuco. "Hombre, your memory is slipping. You told me that one a long time ago. It's Mayan, and it's about a witch who hatches a baby from an egg and raises him as her son."

"Yes! And the baby is very wise, but he stays little all his life. I see you paid attention, Maestro." Cuco smiled broadly, showing off his gums where many teeth were missing.

"To you, Cuco, I always pay attention." The bus came up and stopped with a shriek of its brakes. Rafael touched the brim of his hat to Cuco and climbed aboard. Rafael could not remember when he and the fruit vendor had first began to trade stories. For years and years, probably since the time Rafael remarked on the name painted on Cuco's cart. Over time, Cuco had provided Rafael with two stories that had been new to him. He had added both to the book of Indian legends he was compiling.

The bus lurched away, and Rafael steadied himself and looked around for a seat, but the bus was full, so he stood in the aisle, a hand on the overhead bar, his satchel propped between his legs. Looking out the bus windows, he glimpsed brief flashes of the sea as it showed itself here and there between buildings and houses and huts. Rafael thought of his friends having lunch at the hotel. He thought of home. He wished for once he had gone to the hotel.

At his stop in Santiago, Rafael got off the bus. He went past the bakery, the meat place and the beer and soda depository. All were closed now. He turned the corner and went up the street, past Esperanza Clemente's house and clinic. It, too, was closed for siesta time. Esperanza was a nurse and midwife. Once a week she visited his mother to tend to her rheumatism. The sight of Esperanza was a balm to Rafael. He wanted someday to sit with Esperanza in some beachside restaurant. He did not allow himself to think of what he would have to do for this wish to come true.

Rafael reached his house and went inside. He paused in the narrow passageway that separated his house from the neighboring one. The passageway led to a wide patio that was the home of a mango tree, a flock of speckled chickens and a yellow-eyed cat called Chacbolay. Rafael set his satchel down. He took off his hat and wiped his forehead and the back of his neck with his handkerchief. He felt flushed. Perspiration dampened his shirt. He leaned against the wall of the house, shaken suddenly by the heat and the predictabilities of his life. In a moment his mother would appear. *"Buenas, Maestro,"* she would say, and there would be that little titter in her voice, that coy look in her eye. She would hurry to him, her enormous girth shifting inside one of the black tent-like dresses she insisted on wearing. "The good son returns," she would say before plucking up his satchel.

Rafael Beltrán waited for his mother, but she did not appear. After a moment, he put his hat back on and went into the patio. "Mamá," he called. When there was no response, he stepped up onto the veranda that ran along the back of the house. He poked his head into the living room and into his bedroom and then into his mother's room. There was no sign of her.

Anxiety blossomed in the center of his chest. He crossed the patio where the chickens pecked aimlessly along the ground and the cat lay stretched along a branch of the mango tree. He hurried to the kitchen, and there was his mother, doña Lina. Her back was to the door. She was speaking to a young girl Rafael had never seen before.

"¿Mamá?"

Doña Lina turned around. A little look of surprise crossed her face. "You're home, and I didn't come to greet you." She hurried to him, wiping her hands on her apron. "Here. Let me take your things." She stopped short. "Where's your satchel?"

"Back there." Rafael motioned toward the patio. "I'll get it in a moment." He looked past his mother at the girl. She's Nahuatl, he thought, seeing her Indian lineage in her dark color and the roundness of her face. The girl did not avert her eyes when he looked in her direction.

"I'll get your things," doña Lina said. She left the kitchen and Rafael followed. They were in the patio when he asked, "Who is the girl? Why is she here?"

"That's Inés. She's going to help with the cooking. My hands, you know." She lifted her rheumatic hands to Rafael as if she were a surgeon approaching an operating table. "I told you about her, remember?"

"No, I don't remember."

"Well, I told you. Here, let me have your hat." She made a little explosive sound with her mouth that showed her exasperation. "And take off that shirt. It's all wet."

Rafael ignored his mother. He went to collect his satchel.

"Well, I did tell you, but you never listen." Doña Lina hastened along beside him. "She'll come each weekday to make lunch and stay until dinner is started. I'll pay her out of the money your brothers send. I don't need to give her much. She's just a little Indian girl."

The remark irritated Rafael, but he said nothing. He recalled the old language texts and the workbooks he'd used at school. In them, Indians were pictured as poor and humble outsiders whom mestizo children should treat kindly.

"The girl hasn't lived here long," doña Lina went on. "She says she's from Hueyapan. Padre Juan, at the church, sent her to me."

Hueyapan. It was a town near the capital. The town's population was heavily Indian. Xochimilca

Indians. Not Nahuatl. Rafael bent over his satchel. He pushed his mother's hands away.

"*¿Cuántos años tiene?*"

"*¿Qué?*"

"*La muchacha. ¿Cuántos años tiene?*"

"She's fourteen."

"She should be in school," Rafael said. He picked up his satchel and walked away from his mother.

* * *

When he came home for lunch, Rafael and his mother would eat in the dining room at the end of the veranda, next to the kitchen. Now Inés served these meals. Usually it was a tureen of soup, then a piece of fish or meat and an assortment of vegetables. Over the days, Rafael guardedly watched the girl go back and forth from kitchen to table with dishes and platters and trays. He discerned an air of moodiness about her. He saw it in the way she swung open the kitchen door with a thrust of the hip or in the hasty way she set down a dish. Curiously, this sullenness did not show itself on her face which was always serious and impassive. It was as if something smoldered inside the girl. Something taking its time to surface.

"*La indita es muy buena,*" doña Lina said a few weeks after Inés had arrived, when the girl was in the kitchen, out of earshot. Doña Lina sat at the head of the table, her great chest puffed out. "We have your brothers to thank for this."

Rafael made no response to his mother's last comment. The truth was that, though his brothers were faithful in sending money, the two of them— both in their early fifties, one living in Mexico City, the other in Veracruz—had not visited Santiago in over five years. Periodically, each sent for their mother for a few weeks' vacation, and this allowed Rafael some time to himself. They were both very proud, they said, of the devotion Rafael showed their mother.

"I wish you wouldn't call the girl that," Rafael said.

"What do you mean?"

"*Indita.* You know it's derogatory."

Doña Lina said, "Well, I don't call her that to her face. And anyway, she *is* Indian, isn't she?"

"That appears to be true." Rafael drank down his coffee and pushed his cup away. He folded his napkin and placed it next to his plate. He got up from the table.

Doña Lina turned her arm and looked at her watch. "*Es hora de mi novela,*" she said, pushing back her chair. For months she had been listening to a drama on the radio entitled "The Right to Be Born." At siesta time all Santiago seemed to be tuned to it. Rafael was thankful for the respite. He could always count on a little peace while the program was on.

Rafael picked up the newspaper he'd set aside to read and went out into the patio. He had an hour before going back to school, and he liked to spend it under the mango tree, relaxing in the chair with the flat wooden armrests. His mother settled herself in the easy chair on the veranda. She turned on the radio, and soon a saccharine swell of music announced the program's beginning. Rafael unfolded his newspaper from Mexico City. He took it twice a week to keep up with events. He looked over the headlines. The minister of the interior was accused of graft. The president had scheduled a trip to Guadalajara. Rafael glanced up from the paper. The girl had come out of the kitchen. She looked quickly toward doña Lina, then she slipped off the veranda and crossed the patio toward Rafael.

She wore a light blue dress with sleeves that were puffed at the shoulders. Her black hair was plaited into two braids that fell over her breasts. Rafael looked in his mother's direction. Sobs came from the radio, and doña Lina chewed on her lower lip. He turned back to the girl, who now stood next to his chair.

"You are a teacher," she said, and Rafael could not be sure if she were asking a question or simply stating a fact.

"*Sí, soy maestro.*"

"I want you to teach me," she said.

Rafael laid his newspaper in his lap. "What is it you want to learn?"

"I don't know how to read. I want to learn to write."

"Have you been to school?"

Inés shook her head, her dark eyes defiant, as if to warn against ill comments.

Rafael regarded her for a moment more before responding. Because he possessed the knowledge to do it, he believed it was his duty to teach her. But it ran deeper than this: he would do it because there was a graveness about her that reminded him of himself.

"I will be happy to teach you," he said.

A smile showed itself at the corners of Inés's mouth, and then quickly vanished. "*Gracias, Maestro,*" she said. "With your permission, I have work to do." Her head held high, she went back across the patio.

For some time after she'd returned to the kitchen, Rafael Beltrán stared at the door through which she'd disappeared. He ran a hand over his face. He glanced over at his mother and was relieved to find her so engrossed in the radio that it appeared she had not noticed his conversation with Inés.

* * *

Rafael Beltrán began to teach Inés to read. Each weekday, while doña Lina listened to the radio, he and Inés sat under the mango tree. Rafael sounded out the alphabet, and she echoed him, her brow furrowed in concentration, her index finger underscoring the large red letters that appeared in the primer he'd brought home for her to use. "These are the vowels," she would say, "ah, eh, ee, oh, oo," and then she would take up her pencil and copy each letter on squares of lined paper, her grip on the pencil so fierce that it caused the tips of her brown fingers to pale. On the day she wrote her name, Rafael clapped his approval as he did with younger students, and Inés clutched the paper to her and beamed at him.

Doña Lina turned away from her program and looked their way. "¿*Qué fue?*" she asked, a distrustful expression on her face.

"Inés has written her name," Rafael said. He went to his mother and showed her the paper on which the block letters that spelled Inés Calzada appeared. But doña Lina looked only cursorily in their direction before turning back to her program. Rafael rejoined the girl, hoping she had not noticed this latest rebuff. Since he'd been teaching her, Rafael had become aware of his mother's disapproval. Rafael had noted that she'd begun to listen to the radio with one ear while training the other toward the mango tree. She displayed her unhappiness with mild barbs that soon dwindled into periods of the stony silence with which he was so familiar.

Tonight, Rafael and doña Lina sat reading on the veranda. The evening was cool. The light of a three-quarter moon filtered through the branches of the tree, stenciling the patio with lacy patterns. Rafael looked up from his book at his mother who was across from him. Caught in the pale light of the lamp at her side, the harsh edges of his mother's temperament appeared soft and transmutable. She was an old woman with no friends. A woman who, except for daily Mass and quick trips to the market, did not venture from her house. Rafael felt a tug of sadness at the pitiable reality of his mother's life. Though for days she had been sullen and uncommunicative, now he decided to draw her out. "The girl, Inés," he said. "She's lucky to be learning where she can be taught. She has you to thank for that, Mamá."

Doña Lina glanced up from her reading. She regarded Rafael for a moment before speaking, "You are right about one thing. I pay *la indita* to work. This is not a school I'm running here."

"She does all the work you ask of her. Teaching her to read only takes a small amount of time. *My* time, I might add." He felt himself bristle.

"I don't know why you bother with her," doña Lina snorted. "She's just a little Indian girl."

"She's bright and she deserves to learn," he said, wishing he had not brought Inés's name up. To dispel his annoyance, he left his chair and walked to the edge of the patio. The chickens were roosting in the tree. He could see them huddled along a lower branch. Chac lay curled in the chair under the tree. He pictured the cat waking and springing on the fowl. He pictured himself taking an aggressive stand against his mother, and almost immediately the thought frightened him.

He remembered back when he was ten. His brother Tomás had moved away to Veracruz. Alfredo had moved two years before. When it was only Rafael who remained at home, his mother had plunged into a mute despair that Rafael was certain he himself had caused. Each day he admonished himself, keeping a mental list of his shortcomings, and all his exhortations, all his little attentions could not prod his mother into speaking.

One day as they sat down to lunch, her silence buzzed so loudly in his head that halfway through his soup he thrust an arm out and sent his soup bowl flying. The outburst stunned him, and he held his breath against the repercussions. But his mother said nothing. She rose from the table, bent over the shards of his shattered bowl and picked up each one, crying softly as she did. He went to her then, because it seemed now he was the cause of yet another of her torments. He hunched down next to her and laid pieces of broken bowl in his own palm. "I am sorry, Mamá," he said, and it was then she spoke. "As well you should be," she had said.

Now Rafael turned back to his mother, who was caught up in her book again. "I'll be in my room," he said, perhaps only to the air around him. He left the veranda, feeling the weighty truth of his existence settling down upon him: he was forty-one, and he lacked something that was intact in other people. He had some biological deficiency that made him a meek and obedient man.

*   *   *

The next morning, a Saturday, Rafael Beltrán took the bus to Manzanillo on his way to El Cerro, the neighborhood where Beto Burgos lived. The boy was a student, and he'd been absent from school again. Rafael planned to get to the bottom of this latest truancy.

It was market day in Manzanillo. Stalls laden with merchandise and roofed with colorful lengths of fabric were set up in the middle of a number of streets. Radios blared, and music and commentary dueled for the ears of passersby. But when Rafael reached El Cerro, all that became changed. Here the morning took on the somberness of the surroundings. El Cerro had no streets, only one unpaved road leading up the hill, past shacks that leaned against their neighbors as if to keep each other from collapsing. And there was no running water in El Cerro except for the spigot at the bottom of the hill. At night, only candlelight would flicker from the shanties. Street lamps lighting the town below would not cast their glow very far up El Cerro's hill.

The hill was steep and Rafael was a little breathless when he came to Beto's house. The house had tarpaper walls and a flat tin roof that in an hour or two would fiercely magnify the heat. Next to the door was the shack's only window. It had a screen, and on the ledge just inside it, there were bottles lined up in a row, each filled with sea shells and bright bits of glass. Rafael knocked on the door. Concha Burgos, Beto's mother, opened it.

"*Buenos dias, Señora.*" Rafael took off his hat and held it against his thigh.

"*Buenas, Maestro,*" she said, not looking at all surprised at seeing him here. She stepped out of the house and closed the door softly behind her. "The boys are sleeping," she said. She was a young woman, in her late twenties perhaps, and there was about her a domesticity that told of a husband and children, and of a sweet intimacy that came with both, and which was like a prize being kept from Rafael.

Rafael set his satchel down near the doorway. It was not his intent to launch immediately into the reason for this visit. Concha knew why he was here. He had been here before, and it was always because of Beto. "Today is the *tianguis,*" Rafael said, pointing down the road toward the market. He thought that this was as good a way as any to start the conversation.

Concha nodded and said no more, and Rafael took this as a cue and spoke up. "Two days last week Beto was not in school."

"The boy was fishing with his father. The fishing is good now, and four hands in the boat are better than two."

"I'm happy that times are good," Rafael said, "but a boy's education is very important." He had said this to her before, and he wished he did not have to say it now, for it sounded pompous and removed, as if he did not understand the reality of their lives and how, when all was said and done, everything depended on how much was in the pocket.

Concha was silent for a moment, and then she said, "Beto is only eight. He's the first of mine to go to school."

"Beto is a good boy," Rafael said. He looked at the row of dreary houses across the road and, between them, the dark slash the sea made way off on the horizon. He wished for a future in which there was more than bleakness for the boy, and then he thought of his own life and how it contained a different kind of bleakness.

"The boys and I, we are going to Oaxaca," Concha said. "We are leaving tomorrow."

"Beto will miss school."

"Beto is not going. He will stay with his father."

"I see," Rafael said, and he was about to comment further when he saw the girl Inés coming up the road. Dumbfounded, he stepped back into the shadow cast by the house's overhanging roof. The girl lugged two plastic buckets that, from the way they tugged at her arms, Rafael guessed were filled with water.

"Oaxaca is my homeplace," Concha was saying. "I have not been there in two years." Rafael smiled and gave a nod. He kept a furtive eye on the girl. She went up the road, her shoulders rounded under the weight of the water. Soon she turned toward a shack set apart from the others. An older man who was certainly her father came out as she approached. "What took you so long?" he bellowed. "I want my coffee." When she went past, he poked her in the shoulder and she stumbled and almost lost her grip on the buckets. Water sloshed over their rims and onto her bare feet, but she regained her balance before hurrying into the shack. The man spat on the ground and then lifted his T-shirt and scratched his belly. He looked in Rafael's direction, then went into the shack again.

Rafael pointed up the road. "That girl," he said.

"They're new. There is just the two of them. The old man is not good to her."

"I can see that," Rafael said. He felt the urge to bound across the road and rescue Inés, but he did not give in to it.

*   *   *

In the weeks that followed, Rafael Beltrán felt a bond with Inés because he had glimpsed into her life, and though he did not tell her what he'd seen that morning in El Cerro, he tried to make up for the injustice she experienced. He fashioned a reading primer of simple stories and legends—stories of valor and fortitude—and she took to them readily, always eager for a new one.

One day late in March, as Inés carried lunch in to the table, the extreme caution with which she held on to a platter of chicken and rice caught Rafael's attention. "Is something wrong?" he asked.

Inés paled and whispered, "*No, Maestro*," before she dropped the dish. It struck the side of the table and tumbled over, hitting the floor tiles with a clatter.

"*¡Madre de Dios!*" doña Lina exclaimed just as a great breath exploded from the girl and she crumpled to the ground.

Rafael flung his chair back. He knelt beside Inés, who lay in a heap, her legs drawn up to her chest. She moaned. Pieces of chicken and yellow rice were strewn on the floor. Rafael brushed aside some of the food. His mother came around the table. Clumsily, she squatted down beside Inés.

The girl cried out. She turned onto her back and drew her legs up, hastily poking the skirt of her dress between them. Blood stained her thighs. There was blood on her dress.

"My God, she's hemorrhaging," doña Lina exclaimed.

"Esperanza," Rafael said. "I'll get her." Grateful

for something to do, he bolted across the veranda, down the passageway and out into the street. Esperanza's door was closed when he arrived there. He was out of breath. His heart thundered in his chest. He banged a fist against the door, and when Esperanza opened it, he said her name and stopped because until now he had not known how relieved he would be to see her.

"Rafa. What's happened?"

"You must come to the house."

Esperanza stepped out onto the sidewalk. "Is it your mother?"

"No. It's the girl, Inés. She's bleeding. I think she's dying." It struck him now that there was so much blood. He looked at his hands as if they too might be bloody.

"I'll get my bag," Esperanza said.

They could hear the girl's cries as they rushed into the house. Inés was lying a short distance from the table now. A dark smear on the floor tiles marked the path over which she'd moved. Doña Lina was still at her side.

Esperanza dropped down beside the girl.

"She's bleeding profusely," doña Lina said. "I wadded a towel between her legs."

Rafael turned away. There was nothing more he could do. He went into his bedroom and closed the door. At his desk, he turned on the lamp and dropped into the chair. He looked at his watch. In less than an hour and a half he was due back in school. He closed his eyes. The girl. What was happening to her? He did not know much about girls. And women? Women were simply a mystery.

He heard the door open and his mother was there. Her expression was grave.

Rafael got up from the chair. It was not good news his mother brought. "Did the girl die?"

Doña Lina closed the door. She stepped halfway across the room. "No, she did not die. *La indita* is far from dead."

"Oh?" He was confused. "I thought that because of the blood . . ."

She did not allow him to finish. "She's having a miscarriage."

"A miscarriage?"

"The girl has been beaten. Obviously by her father. You told me about him, remember? Well, he must have learned she was pregnant and beat her because of it." Doña Lina went to sit on the edge of the bed. The springs creaked in protest. "Actually, Rafael, the man did us a favor."

Rafael shook his head. "A favor?"

"You don't have to worry. I said nothing to Esperanza. But frankly, Rafael, I saw all this coming. *La indita* and you. All those hours under the mango tree. All the conspiring between you. Then those Saturdays when you were gone all morning."

To Rafael it was as if the room had suddenly grown smaller.

"*Mamá*. What are you saying?"

"I'm not naive, Rafael. I'm an old woman. I've lived a long life and have seen many things. Men have needs. I know this. *Inditas* like her, they take advantage. They . . ."

That familiar buzzing sound started up in Rafael's head and he did not hear what else his mother had to say. He laid a hand over his ear and went out the door, reeling a little when he stepped into the brightness of the veranda. He picked up his hat and satchel and headed down the passageway. At the front door, Esperanza caught up with him. "You're leaving?"

Rafael nodded. "I have papers to correct."

"Did your mother tell you about Inés?"

He nodded again.

Esperanza patted Rafael's arm. "You look so serious, but don't worry. Inés will be fine. She's young and resilient. As soon as I can, I'll take her to my house. We can't let her go home. Her husband is very violent. If he comes looking for her, we can't tell him where she is."

"Her husband? She doesn't have a husband." The man who had come out of the shack that morning in El Cerro filled Rafael's mind. "Wasn't it her father who beat her?"

"No, Rafa. It was her husband. The man she lives with is her husband."

"That can't be."

"But it's true. I've talked to the girl. Each week when I come to treat your mother, the girl and I talk. Believe me, I know all about Inés's situation."

Rafael could not think clearly. "Does my mother know?"

"Does she know what?"

"That it was her husband who beat her. Does my mother know that?"

Bewilderment crossed Esperanza's face. "I don't know." She looked toward the patio. "I have to go. When you get back, come to my house. We have to make plans for Inés."

Rafael left the house and caught the bus to Manzanillo. After a while, his muddled mind began to clear. He could not forgive his mother for what she had thought of him. He and the girl. The girl was a child. She was only a few years older than his students. He had been a teacher for sixteen years. He was a good teacher. A good man. Out the bus window, Rafael caught glimpses of the sea as he rode along. He thought, I am the son whose mother never considered him, and for the rest of the afternoon, while he worked at his desk, he could think of little else.

* * *

Later, when Rafael Beltrán got home, his mother intercepted him just inside the door. Doña Lina was not wearing her customary black dress but had on a green one shot through with gold threads. The dress was stretched tight across her chest and middle.

"I have a surprise for you," she said. "*El fotógrafo* is here. We've been waiting for you. He's going to take our photograph." She turned an awkward pirouette. "I pulled this out of the back of the closet. It suits me, don't you think?"

Rafael did not greet his mother. He did not stop, but continued on toward the veranda.

Doña Lina came puffing up behind him and fell into step. "You're angry with me," she said, "I can see it. Well, can you blame me? I know now the girl is married. Esperanza told me. I know now it wasn't you, but it could have been. Girls like that often take advantage."

Rafael stepped up onto the veranda. There was a large box camera sitting on a tripod next to his mother's easy chair. An opened suitcase filled with film and colorful objects lay on the floor. Next to the camera stood a man wearing a gray hat. He had on a shiny suit coat with a weary red carnation in the lapel.

"*Muy buenas, Maestro,*" the man said and Rafael thought he heard the man's heels click together. The man strode briskly over and extended a hand to Rafael. "Fulgencio Llanos at your service."

Rafael took the man's hand and nodded. His mother hurried over. "El Señor Llanos is very well known. He is the one who photographed El Santo without his mask."

"*La Tribuna* carried the photos," the photographer said, rocking back a little on his heels when he said this.

Rafael vaguely remembered seeing something about El Santo many months before. Wrestling was not a sport that interested him.

"El Señor Llanos is going to take our photograph," doña Lina said. Her face was moist and flushed. With a finger she wiped away a line of perspiration that had broken out over her lip. "We will send the portraits to your brothers. It will be the perfect Christmas gift."

"I have to go out," Rafael said and headed for his room. He hung up his hat and placed his satchel on his desk. He heard his mother out on the veranda. "I didn't know my son had other plans," she said. "Maybe you should come back another time."

"But Señora, you look so lovely. That dress compliments perfectly your handsome features. Surely you would want me to capture the moment and your loveliness in a photograph."

"I think you should come back," doña Lina said. "Come back some other time when my son can be here."

"But I am a busy man, Señora. I do not know when I'll be back this way again. Seize the moment, Señora. Seize the moment now."

Rafael went into the bathroom, undressed and showered. In his room again, he put on fresh clothing.

His mother was in the patio when he came out. The photographer and his equipment were gone. Doña Lina hastened over. "I sent *el fotógrafo* away," she said. "I don't want a photograph without you in it." When Rafael made no response, she asked, "Where are you going?"

"Out," he said, starting for the door.

She followed him back down the passageway. "Is this the way a son should treat his mother? I demand some respect, Rafael."

Rafael went out the door. He did not look back. When he reached Esperanza's house, they went to sit in Esperanza's front room which also served as a waiting room for her clients. There were no clients at this hour. It was only she and Rafael.

"You didn't wear your hat," Esperanza said.

Rafael ran a hand over his head. "I must have forgotten it." Esperanza had changed into a different dress than the one she'd worn this morning. This one was white and had tiny red flowers printed over it. "I like the little flowers on your dress," he said.

Esperanza poked her chin into her chest and looked down at herself. "They're not flowers. They're stars. But you can call them flowers if you want." She laughed, showing her two front teeth, which were slightly crooked.

"Do you want to have coffee? We can go to the café down the street."

She frowned. "I can't. I don't want to leave Inés. She had a hard afternoon. But I can make coffee and we can have some here. I even have some pastries."

"That would be nice," Rafael said. "Will Inés be all right?"

"Oh, yes. Soon life will be very different for Inés. I phoned a couple I know in Guadalajara. They'll take Inés in. She leaves tomorrow, on the eight o'clock bus."

"Everyone needs a new beginning," Rafael said.

*   *   *

The next day, before school started, the three stood at the bus stop and waited for Inés's bus. Others waited too. The morning was still cool, the sunlight weak and diffused. Inés stood beside Esperanza, leaning on her a bit. The girl was pale. She wore a dress and a pink sweater with pearly buttons down the front that Esperanza had found for her. Inés held a plastic bag that contained a change of clothing and the money Rafael had given her.

The bus came up and people made a run for it. Most carried plastic bags as Inés did, while a few toted suitcases. Rafael watched Esperanza and the girl embrace. When they spoke quietly to each other, Rafael turned his eyes away.

"*Maestro,*" Inés said. She was at his side now, and she had that graveness about her that he would not forget. She laid a hand on his sleeve and then quickly retracted it.

In a moment of inspiration, he opened up his satchel, removed his papers and held out the empty satchel to Inés. "I want you to take it. I'd be proud for you to have it." Gently, Rafael took the plastic bag from her and placed it inside the satchel. He buckled up the straps and pressed the satchel on her.

Inés smiled. For an instant, her face took on that same softness he had seen the day he agreed to teach her. She held the gift close. "*Gracias, Maestro,*" she said and then she turned and ran to join the others on the bus.

With Esperanza beside him, Rafael Beltrán watched the bus pull away. He raised a hand of farewell to the somber face framed in the back window.

Chapter 8

César Burgos

El Pescador
(pescador, n.m. fisherman)

César Burgos awakened very early. For a moment he lay in bed, catching the pitch of the wind and watching a slant of sorry light steal in under the door. "Beto," he whispered, drawing out his son's name, hoping to rouse the boy and trick him into a sleepy response. César was not above such tactics. He wanted his son to speak again. He wanted more from him than a grunt or a shrug. "Beto," César said again, but no answer came from across the room.

César swung himself up. He grabbed his trousers and tugged them on. He shook out his shoes for insect stowaways before slipping into them. The floor was cold, and in the room there was a chill that out at sea would send the fish deep. César pulled on a sweater. He stepped around his son's cot. The eight year old was tucked into a ball. The rebozo that had been his mother's, and that since her death he always took to bed with him, was pulled entirely over his head.

Going to the window, César lifted the curtain. The morning was gray. Little whirlwinds skipped along the road. César let the curtain drop and went across the room. At the stove, he lit its two burners. On one he placed the coffee pot he'd readied the night before. When the coffee grew hot, he poured a cup. Behind him his son stirred. César turned to him. Beto was propped up on an elbow. He had pulled the shawl down tight around his shoulders. He was dark, like his mother, with the same bow of a mouth that had been hers. "Did you sleep?" César asked.

Beto shrugged. He sank back onto the cot, drawing the rebozo over his head once more.

César stared at the boy enshrouded in the length of cloth that still contained his mother's scent. He thought about the way things had been before the day misfortune struck. Despite the shifting tides of a life dependent on the sea, he had been a man who lacked little: he had possessed a humble house, the companionship of a woman, good and true, and, above all, three sons, on whom he'd rested much of his hopes for the future.

César sipped his coffee. It was a Saturday, the start of norther season, and the sea was choppy. On days like this ocean fishing was not good, and César would take to estuaries where he knew the fish to be. Still, despite the weather, he would put out to sea today. Today, he needed the sea under him. Each time he stepped into his boat, he left his heartbreak on the shore. In his boat, he was shielded from the monstrous turn his life had taken.

"I want you out of bed," César said. He turned back to the stove, hearing the sternness in his voice that was his way of holding on. He removed the coffee from the burner and set a pot of beans on it. He lowered the flame on the second burner and laid three tortillas around it. This had been Concha's life. She fixed the meals and went to market. She kept the house swept and dusted. She cared for the children.

Now it was he who had to tend the house and raise the one son he had left. In the two months since the accident he had done these things and gone to sea as well. He was doing a terrible job of it. The sea was so demanding that from June until November, when the weather was very good, it was fishing, fishing, morning through night, and who could raise a boy well with hours like that. Before he'd turned to fishing, he had done other kinds of work, but he did not want to contemplate leaving the fish when it was the sea that served him best.

When the tortillas were hot, César plucked them from the flame and stacked them on a plate. He scooped beans on, too, and set the food on the table. Beto had laid aside Concha's rebozo and now sat on the edge of the cot, pulling on the worn pair of Adidas he insisted on wearing without laces. He went over to the dresser and dunked a comb into a glass of water before running the comb through his hair. A tuft at the top of his head would not be tamed despite the effort, but César resisted the urge to point this out to the boy. Beto poured a cup of coffee and padded over to the table. "Coffee's not good for you," César said. "There's milk there."

Beto took a gulp of coffee. He screwed up his face against the taste of it.

César bit his lip. At school the boy was sullen and uncommunicative. When his mother and little brothers were alive, he was a different kind of boy. *Chinga,* César thought, who wasn't different then. They had been a happy family. Rodolfo and Reynaldo were curious, bubbly boys who loved their big brother and looked up to him. Beto was protective of them. When they got into mischief, he'd step between them and Concha if she picked up the broom and laughingly come after them. Frequently the three sat on Beto's cot, all propped against the wall, and Beto spilled out the seashells he collected. He told the boys stories. How this spotted shell had come from this place in the sea. How this small conch had left behind his brothers and how, if the boys placed the shell against their ears, they could hear the other shells calling. Now César glanced over at the window ledge on which Beto had kept the jars containing his collection. Sometime after the accident—César had not noticed exactly when—the jars had disappeared.

"Please eat your breakfast," he said to the boy.

Beto pushed his plate away.

"You must eat," César said, the edge of frustration building in his voice because right before his eyes the boy was languishing. To get a grip on himself, César turned his attention to the shrine that occupied the better part of the table. If the shrine was ever finished, he would place it on the side of the road at the spot where the bus speeding back from Oaxaca had not made the curve.

The shrine was a large square box built to resemble a chapel. It had a glass door in front, and on the top, over the door, a tall wooden cross. César Burgos had worked on the shrine for nearly a month, but every attempt he'd made to enhance it had failed somehow. He had painted the shrine pink, and then a blue like an early sky. Now it was white, and as he ran a hand over it, its plainness distressed him. He had asked his son for help, but the boy had refused.

César left the table and the dismal sight of the shrine and his son. He went to the window and looked out again. The wind had died down, but the sky was still gray. Between the shacks across the street, the sea was a dark smear, but still the sight of it was comforting. He loved the grandness of the sea, the formidable mystery it presented. He loved the creatures of the sea, those he saw and those he could only imagine. When he'd first arrived in Manzanillo—

he had been born in the capital, but had left it for Veracruz and the sugar cane fields there—he had fished from the shore with harpoon and net, but later, when he had a skiff, he'd go out to sea. Each day he'd sit in his boat and chase the fish and savor his freedom, for there was freedom in fishing. Not so with the sugar cane. Fishing gave a man the time to think in silence. It brought the feel of water and its movement, the sight of the colors that played over it. It brought sky and clouds, sunlight and moonlight glimmering on the mountains or along the shore. Fishing brought perils, too. Peril from tides and winds and from the sea's creatures. But peril heightened vigilance. Peril provided the situation against which a man could test his mettle. Twelve years ago, when he was nineteen, he'd first come upon this sea. He had left Veracruz and crossed the width of Mexico to come to Manzanillo. Here he faced a new sea, and it took months to learn the peculiarities of tides and currents, to memorize the distances, the placement of rocks and, sometimes, of trees that served to mark certain depths or fishing spots. And the winds here were unlike the winds on the other coast of Mexico, and they affected these fish differently, and so there was that too he had to learn. But the stars above him had not changed, and it was a blessing to look up into the night and know the stars had followed him through all the journeys of his life.

When he was twenty-one, he had married Concha Ojeda. It was she who had allowed him to turn himself over to the sea. But now Concha was gone and in the months since the accident, the boy had gone mute and was clearly in decline. The boy needed a mother's love, he needed a father's strength, and there was none of one and little left of the other. César thought of Concha's sister, who lived in Oaxaca. She had asked for the boy. She would raise him with her own, she had said at the wake. Since that time, César Burgos had agonized over his sister-in-law's offer and there were moments when he thought he would have to let the boy go.

He turned to his son, who sat at the table, his chin dropped down onto his chest. "After a while, we'll go out on the sea," César said. Since the accident, the boy had rejected going out in the boat. But today César would insist. Perhaps the sea might turn the boy into himself again.

Beto said nothing.

"Did you hear what I said. I said we'll go out on the boat."

Still no response came from his son.

"Why don't you speak?" César cried, heat surging up his neck and into his cheeks. "In God's name, say something, say anything!"

Beto slumped into the chair.

César pressed the back of his neck, a sense of helplessness washing over him. He turned his gaze out the window again. There is nothing I can do for my son, he thought. *Nada. Absolutamente nada.*

*   *   *

Out on the boat, the sea was leaden. There were times when the sea was very blue and the water was silky to the touch and it gleamed and you could look down into it, seeing quite clearly the fishing nets ballooning down into the deep, seeing the schools of haddock or sea bass or dogfish heading in a silent rush for the nets. But today the north wind threatened, and the sea was dense, and you could not look past its surface. Overhead the sky was mottled, and soon fat raindrops fell, tiny craters forming where they struck the water. César Burgos ignored the rain. He sat in the stern of his boat, his eyes on his son's back. Beto's shirt collar poked out from his sweater and curved like a wide red petal around his neck. The boy's neck is like Concha's,

César thought, and he looked away, toward the buildings that were staggered up the slope close to the shore. On some of these buildings' balconies tiny red and green lights twinkled. Christmas, he thought, Concha's best time and it was almost here again. César clutched the sides of the boat, remembering past Christmases, remembering the aroma of *pozole* and *empanadas,* the star piñata he hung from a tree branch in the yard, the fireworks lighting up the night sky of Manzanillo.

At the memories, the grief pent-up inside César spilled out and he began to weep. Since the accident, he had not allowed himself to weep, for a man must be strong. But now images of his lost sons and the pudgy flesh between their soft knuckles, images of Concha and the silent, hungry way she sometimes turned to him in the night broke his restraint. César cried out and he heard the sound he made. Though he felt the warmth of tears against his face, he could not hold his grief back.

César did not know how long it was before he felt the boat bobble. He opened his eyes and saw that Beto had turned around. Now his son planted his feet wide to steady them. In Beto's eyes his own despair shone out.

César wiped his tears with the heel of a hand. "I can't seem to make things right," he said. "I've tried to be a mother to you, a father too, but I have failed. I'm afraid for you, and I'm afraid for me. You are slipping away. First it was your voice and now it's the rest of you, and there is nothing I can do. Your tía Bersa, in Oaxaca, has offered to take you. I think of this sometimes and now I think it would be good if you went to live with them." César went silent, because the weight of his confession was like he'd dropped an anchor out.

Beto opened his mouth as if he would speak, but he

did not. Instead, he shook his head. It was a slow, sad movement that tore open César's heart. César closed his arms around the boy and pressed him to his chest. "*M'hijo*," he said finally, murmuring against the boy's head, using the words "my son" because it was what his mother always called him.

*   *   *

It was raining in earnest when the two reached home. They had rowed the boat in, dragged it up on shore, turning the boat over next to others secured in the sandy yard of the fishing cooperative. The two were soaked when they stepped into their house. César lighted a few candles, for the morning had gone dark. He turned on both stove burners to allow a little heat into the room. He and Beto changed into dry clothes and then César made fresh coffee. For the boy, he made chocolate, boiling up the water, dropping in a tablet of good Oaxacan chocolate, whipping up the mixture with the wooden beater just like Concha used to do. César brought the filled cups to the table, and the two sipped their drinks while the downpour beat an endless drumroll against the roof.

After a time, César dragged out a fishing net and the canvas bag that held his mending tools. The din the rain made was soothing, a perfect accompaniment to net mending. César selected a few lead weights and began to sew them into the rim of a turquoise net where some were missing. Soon after, Beto went to his cot and pulled three glass jars out from underneath. He carried the jars over and spilled his collection of seashells onto the table. César was amazed.

Beto went to the dresser and took out the balsa wood boat model and the tube of cement *el maestro* had given him after the funeral. The gift had gone untouched, but now Beto brought the glue to the table and lifted the cloth covering the shrine. He began to glue seashells to the outer surface of the box.

Concha! César thought, the word that meant "seashell." César laid down his own work and joined the boy who did not object.

A few hours later, when they were finished, the two stood and admired how it was they had elevated a mere box and cross into a proper shrine. Now the shrine was studded with turret shells and milky limpets. Glued on too were miniature horn shells in chestnut and violet, fig shells and auger shells in hazel and cream. Still, though the overall effect was splendid, there were gaps between the shells that needed filling in. "It needs something more," César said, pointing to the gaps.

Beto jumped up. He ran to his cot again and brought out another jar. He hurried back and turned the jar over. It was as if the boy had scattered jewels upon the table. What once had been bottle shards time and the sea had polished into gems. There were amber and aqua and rose colored nuggets. Nuggets as green as a wild parrot's wing. Nuggets as clear and as dazzling as diamonds. Until his mother's death, it had been the boy's greatest pleasure to stroll up and down the beach, his dark head bent in search of such miraculous transformations.

Beto selected a green nugget and fitted it between two seashells, holding it in place with his fingertips. He looked up to his father for approval.

"It is the crowning touch," César Burgos said, and for a few hours more he and his son picked over the gems, fixing each one to the spot where the shrine itself seemed to call for it. When their task was done, they both stepped back as if from a distance they could see more keenly. The shrine, faceted now with these polished colored jewels, brightened a room that for months had been drab.

*　　*　　*

It was almost two o'clock when they went out again. Though it had cleared, the daylight was still weak. César and Beto made their way carefully down the steep muddy road that led into Manzanillo. Once there, they caught the bus to Santiago. They were going to buy paper flowers from Chayo Marroquín, who made the best ones sold on the beach. The flowers would go on the inside of the shrine as the final touch.

When they got to Chayo's house, she was at the stove, making lunch. Because of the weather, Candelario was home too. He stood up from the table when César and Beto appeared at the door. "Hombre," he said to César. On many occasions the two had fished together, and they were as companionable as time spent on the sea permitted men to be. "*Entren, entren,*" Chayo said, wiping her hands on her apron and hurrying over to the door. She was young, in her twenties, yet there was a motherly air about her that made her seem older. The room was warm and brightly lit, filled with the odor of coffee, the sweet pungency of onions and tomatoes frying in a pan. Simply put, there was the aroma of home here, and César Burgos hungrily took it all in. The walls were bright blue. A wide yellow stripe formed a border along the ceiling. From the rafters, bouquets of paper flowers hung down like cornucopias.

"We built a road shrine for Concha and the little ones," César said. "We have come for flowers."

Chayo clapped her hands. "A road shrine. *Qué bueno,*" she said, deftly navigating around the room's happy clutter: the imposing double bed, the awkward dressers, the uneven table and odd matching chairs. Strung in a corner was a hammock within which a baby slept in spite of the noise. Chayo threw a plump arm around Beto, who hung back by the door. "You can have your pick of any of my flowers, but first a little something for the stomach."

César protested, but Chayo turned a deaf ear and soon they were sitting down to a table covered with a stack of hot tortillas and bowls of rice and beans and a platter of sauced green peppers dotted with bits of meat.

César was surprised at how greedily his son and he ate. When they had finished, Chayo removed the plates. "And now to the flowers," she said, pointing out the room with a sweep of her hand. César Burgos stood. He looked around. There was a garden of blossoms here—how could he settle on just the right ones? "Beto, you decide," he said. "I'll be outside." He left hastily because the room began suddenly to close in on him. He did not know why, perhaps he needed the spread of sky. Perhaps it was air he needed, though out in the yard the blessed smell of salt was hardly in it. He went to stand next to the arroyo. After a time, Candelario walked up. "So you finished the shrine."

"Yes. We'll put it up Christmas Eve. Concha always made so much of that day."

There was silence, because in silence there was more respect than in any words that they could say.

"How are you going?" Candelario asked at length.

"*¿Que?*"

"How will you get it there, you know, the shrine?"

César reeled at the question. The place of the accident was a good ten kilometers away. The shrine was awkward, heavy. He hadn't thought of how he would carry it. He felt like a fool. "The bus? The bus goes past there." He said this, but he couldn't bear to think about him and the boy and the shrine on the bus.

Candelario pointed next door. "Santos is my neighbor. He has a taxi. Santos can take you."

"*Ay, hombre, tomar un taxi es muy caro.*" César

Burgos could not afford to take a taxi. Only once in his life had he done it, and that was on his wedding day.

Candelario laid a hand on César's sleeve. "No, hombre. Santos is a good man. He's reasonable. I'll arrange for it."

"*Gracias, hombre. La verdad, mi vida es una pura mierda.*"

*   *   *

César Burgos and his boy stood on what looked like the top of the world. They were on a wide shoulder that bordered the road to Oaxaca, a road of switchbacks and long curves. At the road's edge, the terrain tumbled, forming a ravine from which spindly pines and shrubs sprouted. As if to soften its severity, clumps of yellow flowers poked up here and there down the *barranca*.

It was early and the sky was a blue so brilliant that it looked like the sea.

Minutes before Santos had dropped them off. The man had helped to heft the shrine from the taxi's trunk and place it next to a thicket of young trees. When César dug into his pocket, Santos said, "No, hombre. Let a man do a man a favor." He had clasped César in an awkward embrace before driving off as it was planned that he would. César was thankful for Santos's kindness. He was thankful, too, to be here alone with his son.

Beto backed away from the ravine. He had not been here before. He had worn his dark cloth coat because there was a chill and because it was the most formal thing he had to wear. Over his shoulder lay the pack in which he usually carried his school books.

"It's very deep," César Burgos said, because he had twice trudged the depth and breadth of the *barranca,* once just after the accident, and then again on the day he came to fix the spot where the shrine would sit.

Now he looked out past the edge of the road to the place where officials said the bus had left the curve. In his mind he saw the bus. He saw it sail out into an emptiness he could not bear to think his loved ones had had the time to face. "We should get started," he said.

They hoisted the shrine up, carrying it to the base on which it would rest. The base was a simple concrete pedestal standing among sturdy cement shrines, crosses and a few plaques. They lowered the shrine onto the pedestal, guiding the bottom of it carefully over the short rods that would anchor it.

"It looks very good," César said when at last the shrine was set. Behind the glass door, his wife's face looked out at him. She was somber in the photograph, her jet eyes steady, as if somehow back then she had understood what was to come. At each side of her was a photograph of a boy: three-year-old Rodolfo and four-year-old Reynaldo. A wreath of paper flowers trailed around the photographs, and the arch of the petals, the pinks and blues and violets, softened the graveness of the three faces.

Beto lowered the pack from his shoulder and took from it a parcel of folded cloth that César recognized as Concha's rebozo. It was black with crimson threads running through it. She had woven the shawl herself, had worn it for the first time on her wedding day. When the boys were babies, she had wrapped each one of them in it, cradled them in it against her heart.

Beto carried the rebozo over to the shrine as if it were an offering. Solemnly he draped it over one side of the shrine and up and around the cross and then down the other side.

César was perplexed by what his son had done, but before he could question him, Beto knelt before the shrine and began to speak. His voice was soft and slow. "Mamá," he said, "I brought you your rebozo because I don't deserve to have it. I should have gone with you, Mamá. You wanted me with you in Oaxaca. You wanted me to help you with the little ones, but I said no because *el maestro* does not like it when I don't come to school. But I was wrong to say no, Mamá. If I had gone, I would have saved my brothers. It was up to me to do it, but I was not there and so Naldo and Rody died. It was my fault, Mamá. *Yo tuve la culpa.*" Beto, the small penitent, lowered his head.

César was thunderstruck by what he had heard. He dropped down next to his son. "*No, hijo, no,*" César said. "*No tuviste la culpa.*"

"But I stayed home. It *was* my fault. If I had gone, I could have saved them."

"*No, hijo.* No one could have saved them. Everybody died in that crash. *Todos, hijo, todos.*"

As if pondering what César had said, Beto was silent for an instant, but then he spoke again, "Then I should have gone with them. If I had gone I would be dead too." He spoke haltingly, as if he had a measured number of words and they were soon to run out. "If I was dead now, I wouldn't be a bother to you, Papá."

César Burgos pulled Beto close and then drew away just enough to look into his eyes. "You are not a bother. You are my son. You are all I have in the world and I never want to lose you."

Beto buried his face against his father's chest.

"Come," César said after a moment. He stood and brushed at the bits of gravel clinging to the knees of his trousers. He went to the shrine and lifted his wife's rebozo, careful not to catch it on the seashells. He folded the cloth that was as soft as Concha's skin. "This is yours. Your mother would want you to have it now." He handed the rebozo back to his son.

Beto gave a little nod. He returned the shawl to his pack again and then stood beside his father.

"Concha would be proud," César Burgos said. He

pictured the sea and his boat. And he pictured his son as a help to him in the future. César Burgos laid an arm across his boy's shoulders. They started off, toward the point down the road where the bus always stopped.

Chapter 9

Remedios Elementales: Agua

(agua, n.f. water)

Toward sunset, Remedios slips from her hut and hurries down the winding road that leads to the sea. Once there she sits on her heels, her feet set wide apart and steady. All her life it has been this: herself a stone so near blue water.

Remedios's heart brims with stories. Day after day, people trudge up the hill to her. Few she turns away. She knows people's dreams, people's secrets. She knows their burdens, their grief.

In her hut, Remedios listens to someone's story, and the teller is revived.

It is stories that save us, Remedios is certain.

A breeze starts up and the sun is low over the water. Sea foam rolls toward shore and is gently chased away. Holding on and letting go. It is one of the sea's duties. Remedios's duty is to come here for her own renewal. Today her heart is very heavy. People's stories take a toll.

Remedios fixes her gaze and catches the flash of the setting sun. She sees in it the iridescence of a bird's wing. *Urraca,* her familiar, flies now to her.

Fortified by the salted air, her spirit and the bird soar up over blue. Gulls shriek their greeting. Waves break a welcome over rocky promontories. The vanishing sun lays a crimson path along the water. Urra, urra, *Urraca* cries before gliding back to shore.

Abuela Luna, Grandmother Moon, blossoms, hesitant and pale. Around it, stars are sugared. Remedios reaches for the foamy sea rippling toward her. She touches a finger to her tongue and her own story comes. The sea listens and remembers. So it is the sea preserves.

10

Justo Flores

El Pajarero
(pajarero, n.m. birdman)

Don Justo Flores crossed the patio of his rooming house as the morning began to brighten and turn hot. Yoyo, his German shepherd, lumbered along beside him. The two had been to Lupe Bustos's eatery and Lupe's bracing coffee had warmed the old man's bones, setting his mind on the pluses in life and not on the minuses, as in the days when it was pulque or tequila for breakfast instead of *frijoles con tortillas y café*. Don Justo opened the door to his room and hurried over to the bird cage that hung from the stand in the corner. Yoyo, who at thirteen was always the faithful one, plopped down near the door, while don Justo, with a flourish, pulled the cloth from the cage and uncovered his birds. He owned three canaries: an apricot pair named Romeo and Julieta and, the pride of the bunch, a crested yellow hen called Rita.

Don Justo opened the cage door and the birds fluffed up their feathers and hopped down from their perch. "Come, little beauties," he cooed, and the birds queued up at the opened door just as they'd been trained to do, with Rita at the head of the line because she was the favorite. The canaries moved their heads from side to side and fixed don Justo with eyes as black and glistening as papaya seeds. Next to Yoyo, he loved the birds best. The four were like his family, and it was a comfort to share his life with such sweet and attentive kind. His real family lived in Guadalajara. He'd left them years ago, when their bickering and backbiting had grown too much for him.

"*Rita bonita,*" don Justo said. He tapped his shoulder, and Rita fluttered over and landed near his chin. "*Dame un beso.*" He puckered up his lips and Rita softly pecked them, bobbing her head and joggling the brown tuft of feathers that crowned it. Don Justo offered Rita his finger and she hopped on. He extended his arm and she sprang off to fly in fits and starts because her wings had been clipped to keep her from soaring. Don Justo busied himself with the other birds, and soon they too darted and dipped about the room. Yoyo regarded the birds' antics. He barked and snapped at the air when the birds flew close, but they were used to the dog and were not frightened by his complaints.

In addition to companionship, the canaries were don Justo's only source of income. He was a *pajarero,* a birdman, and each day around ten, he and Yoyo and the birds headed for the beach, where don Justo set up the cardboard castle in which the birds performed. People paid to watch them do tricks. They paid for the printed fortunes Rita selected with her beak.

Don Justo cleaned out the cage and poured fresh water for the birds. He filled their dishes with seed and then he clapped twice. The birds flew into the cage and hopped over to their breakfasts. He was fastening the cage when a knock came at the door. He opened the door to a short man with a thin mustache.

The man wore a uniform and on his head sat a cap sporting a metal badge at its crown. Don Justo stepped back into the safety of his room.

"*¿Don Justo Flores?*" the man inquired. He kept an eye on Yoyo, who was sniffing in the direction of his shoes.

"*¿Sí?*" Don Justo peered out onto the patio as though someone there might explain the man's presence.

"*Telegrama.*" The man extended an envelope to don Justo, who took it, hooking a finger into his pocket for some change. The man plucked up the pesos and walked quickly away.

Don Justo closed the door and leaned against it. Yoyo was at his feet, looking up as if for answers. Don Justo gazed down at the envelope. It was creamy yellow, and it had a narrow window of cellophane under which the telegram showed. Don Justo held the envelope against his chest because in his seventy years there had never been a telegram addressed to him. The sight of one now, the feel of it against his shirt, frightened him.

He went over to the bed and sat on the edge of it. A memory of his mother came to him. She was sitting on a bed, in some place he could not now recall. She was holding a telegram. Don Justo searched his mind for the news it had contained, but he could not say what it had been. All he remembered was that he'd been six, seven perhaps, and it was a telegram that had started the downward plunge that had taken his mother from him.

Don Justo left the room to see if his neighbor, Luz Gamboa, might still be home. Luz was usually at work by now, but if she were home, Luz could read it for him. Luz's husband, Tito, had gone off for good, and Luz bought fortunes from don Justo and read them on the spot in a whispery voice.

Don Justo went across the patio, but just as he'd suspected, Luz was not home. He sat on the stool beside her door. Yoyo, who'd tagged along, gave a moan and lay down at his feet. Don Justo rubbed the dog's flank with the tip of his shoe. He had folded the telegram and put it in his trouser pocket, and the envelope crackled when he moved his leg. The sound was a reproach that said: What have you done with your life, old man, that now comes trouble and you're too ignorant to read what it might be.

He'd had a family once. Over the years, he'd had two wives and nine children. Of the five children who had survived, he'd kept track of only two: Justina, his first, born with the twisted foot, and Ernestina, his fifth. Both lived in Guadalajara, a day's bus ride away. He had made the trip three months before, when he'd gone to stock up on new fortunes and to see Ernestina. He had sat at her table, sharing a pot of coffee, and he had told her about moving to Santiago and about the bird business there. He had asked whether, now that so much time had passed, Justina might see him. "I'm an old man," he had said. "Years go by. Things change. Maybe your sister will take pity on me now." But Ernestina's only answer had been to look down into her cup.

Today don Justo's gaze swept across the doors of the rooms that ringed the patio. He searched for someone who might read for him. A few children played near the toilet shack. At the water spigot two women filled bright plastic pails. Don Justo knew the women only to say hello, so he would not think to ask them for help. He thought of Marta Rodríguez, his next-door neighbor, but Marta worked at the hotel and so she too was not likely to be home. Besides, even if she were, Marta lived with her son and an aunt, *la tía Fina*. The old woman was meddlesome and talkative, and the last thing don Justo wanted was *la tía* catching a glimpse into his personal life. No, he'd have to wait for Luz to learn what fate held for him. He stood and nudged the dog with his foot again. "*Vamos, Yoyo. Ya es hora.*" It was time to leave for the beach.

He had almost made it through his door, when *la tía* came out of hers. "*Buenas, Don Justo,*" she said. Richard, Marta's one-year-old, straddled her hip. The boy's name was pronounced "ree-char," after Richard Burton, twice the husband of Elizabeth Taylor, Marta's favorite movie star. All this don Justo had learned from *la tía* herself. Richard was a large boy, with smoldering eyes and dark curly hair. He was a shy child who did not roam too far from his mother's or *la tía*'s side.

"*Buenas, Doña Fina,*" don Justo said, putting on a pleasant smile. Yoyo went up and sniffed around the old woman's legs. Richard shrank back at the sight of the dog. He laid his head against his great-aunt's shoulder.

"Yoyo won't harm you," don Justo said, going over. "He's an old dog. He's as old as me."

"*Richard es un miedoso,*" tía Fina said. "He's afraid of everything."

Yes, don Justo thought. He was fearful too of the news inside his pocket. "It's almost ten. I have to go to work." He said this because he wanted to get going. Today, more than ever, he needed his work to distract him from his fear.

"I should have your Rita pick me out a fortune," *la tía* said. "After the other day, Marta hardly speaks to me. Maybe one of your fortunes would tell me what to do."

"*Quizás,*" don Justo said, dodging her attempt to draw him into one of her rambling conversations. He did not want to talk about what had happened the other day. He had been in his room, the door open to a breeze, when Chayo, Marta's sister, stormed into the *mesón*. Tonito, Chayo's son, was with her. Marta was home alone—she had just returned from work—but soon *la tía* rushed in with Richard. Don Justo had not needed to leave his room to know what was happening. It appeared tía Fina had confessed to Chayo—it was her moral obligation to do so, she said—that before Tonito was born, Marta had gone to *el brujo* and placed a curse on him. Chayo ranted and stormed over the news of this betrayal while Marta begged to be forgiven, explaining that she had gone to Remedios to seek the spell's reversal. For proof it was successful, Marta said, wasn't Tonito a hale and hearty boy? But the fact that this was so did not temper Chayo's wrath. "From this day forward, I no longer have a sister," Chayo had pronounced.

During the tirade, don Justo remained in his room while all the neighbors, it seemed, gathered silently in the patio. Next door the drama played itself out: the children wailed and *la tía* explained. Marta pleaded as Chayo raved. To don Justo, it was all very disturbing. Angry words and accusations frightened him. All his life, he had turned away from grief and confrontation. Now, misery was waiting in his pocket and there was no running from it.

"*Es tarde,*" don Justo said. "I have to be going." He managed a cheery wave and slipped quickly into his room. Inside he gathered up the folding stand and the castle in which the birds performed. He filled a pack with a bottle of water and a bag of seed, adding the box of fortunes and the various props the birds used for their tricks. He transferred the birds from their hanging cage to the small one he used to transport them. Rita and Julieta chirped in anticipation of the trip, while Romeo broke out into a clear, sweet song.

At the beach, don Justo found an empty *palapa* and

he and Yoyo hurried under the small thatched shelter. So far he was the only vendor there, and he was glad for the advantage. Few were taking in the sun, though the sea was calm and very green. The waves tumbled gently toward the sunbathers and then rolled out again. The day was hot; the sun glinted fiercely off the white buildings set along the shore. Don Justo opened up the bird stand, thrusting its legs into the sand until it was level. He unfolded the castle—it was constructed in such a way that it, too, could be collapsed—and placed it on the sand. The castle featured two salmon-colored turrets with a yellow platform along the base. A curtain sprinkled with tiny stars hung between the turrets. Don Justo set the tray of fortunes out. He lifted the birds from their cage, placing each on the platform behind the curtain. It troubled him that he must busy himself with this, when something much more pressing needed his attention. The telegram was a nettle in his pocket. Not knowing its contents had soured his stomach. It came to him that a shot of tequila might settle him. On the heels of this thought came another. He had not had a drink for nearly ten years. Ten years and no pulque or tequila. Not even *una cervecita*. He had served his penance, had he not? Ten years to pay for the terrible thing he had done. A splinter of hope wedged ajar the door of despair looming before him. He allowed himself to think that perhaps it was Justina herself who had sent the telegram. He formed a message from her in his mind: "Come home, Papá," the telegram would read. "All is forgiven."

A young girl walked up. She looked about sixteen. Her hair was very black, almost blue in fact, and she had gathered it up at the sides somehow. She reminded him of Justina. Not her face, but her hair. Justina's hair had that same bluish tint about it.

"*Buenas, Señor,*" the girl said.

Don Justo bowed. "You wish to know your fortune, Señorita?"

"¿*Cuánto?*" she said. A necklace of tiny onyx birds encircled her throat, and when she asked the price, she laid a finger on one of the birds as if it might fly off.

"It is very affordable. One fortune, one thousand pesos."

The girl frowned and looked toward a boy who lay nearby, belly down on the beach. He had flung an arm out at his side and his hand lay palm up, curved like a shell. "Chato," the girl cried out, but the boy did not move. The girl rolled her eyes and cried out again. This time the boy stood and, lowering mirrored sunglasses over his eyes, sauntered over to the *palapa*.

To encourage a sale, don Justo opened the curtain to show the birds lined up between the turrets. The birds were alert because they were beginning to work and they knew that seed awaited them. "You wish to know your fortunes?" don Justo asked the two.

"¿*Cuánto?*" the boy asked, half his face a silver glare. He was not much older than the girl and had the same slenderness of waist as she. He brushed sand from his chest and cocked a narrow hip forward. To don Justo it was as if the past had dropped away and he were seeing himself when he was young.

Don Justo repeated the price and the boy poked a finger into the pocket of his trunks and pulled out some bills. He peeled off a thousand pesos and handed it over. The girl did a little dance.

Pointing to Rita, don Justo set to work. "*Rita bonita,*" he said, and Rita nodded her head so that her crest bobbled. "*Romeo y Julieta,*" he added and the birds rubbed their beaks together in a kiss. "*Ay, qué lindo,*" the girl said.

Don Justo placed Romeo and Julieta on each of the perches he'd built inside the turrets. The birds poked their heads out the turret windows and looked toward each other, and Romeo gave a trill. Don Justo bunched his hands together and rolled his eyes. "*Ah, el amor,*" he proclaimed.

The girl giggled behind a hand. She did not look at the boy.

Don Justo placed the box of fortunes in the center of the platform. He whistled three times, and Rita rose and hovered over the fortunes before plucking one up. Don Justo clapped and Rita flitted to the edge of the stand and landed there. A small blue square was captured in her beak.

"*Su fortuna, Señorita,*" don Justo said, making a sweeping gesture toward the bird.

The girl stepped shyly up. Carefully, she pulled the blue paper from Rita's beak. She unfolded the slip. "Oh, look! It's my life fortune." She hurried over to the boy and they began to read.

Seeing them like this, their heads bent in silent study, was a key that freed don Justo's reticence. He pulled the telegram from his pocket and stepped over to the boy. "*Por favor, léame esto,*" don Justo said, reaching out with the envelope.

The boy lifted his sunglasses until they rested on his head. He pulled his leg back, relaxing the projection of his hip. He took the envelope and spread it open and pulled out the telegram. The girl closed a hand over the blue square of her fortune. Don Justo turned to look at the sea. A boat with a red checkered sail glided along the horizon.

"There is bad news here," the boy said.

"*¿Qué dice?*"

There was a hesitation, then the boy spoke, "It says, 'Come home at once, Papá. Justina is gone from us.' It is signed, 'Ernestina.'"

Out on the sea, the sailboat grew smaller. Patches of conversation from the people down by the water floated up to him. Don Justo nodded and took the telegram from the boy and stuffed it back into his pocket.

"I'm sorry, Señor," the boy said. There was a softness in his eyes and he did not lower his sunglasses to cover it. For a moment the three stood in silence under the *palapa,* then the boy took the girl's hand and they both walked away.

Don Justo sprinkled seed on the cage bottom and placed the birds inside. Nearby, Yoyo was panting. Don Justo took the bottle from his pack and poured water into his hand for the dog to lap up. "*Vamos,*" he said. He gathered up his things and started for town, thinking a little tequila would be good to have just now.

*   *   *

Music blared from a radio out in the patio. It rolled under the door and invaded the room. Don Justo sat in the middle of his bed, propped against the wall. The room was growing dim. The walls seemed to throb to the beat of the music. His belly burned with tequila, yet he was chilled. He pulled at the scratchy blanket heaped near him. In the gloom, he saw Yoyo in the corner.

Don Justo called the dog's name, and after a time, the dog heaved himself up and came over. Yoyo laid his head on the mattress, casting a baleful look don Justo's way. Rita flew over and landed nearby. Don Justo offered her his finger and she hopped on. He brought her close to him.

The look in Rita's eye pinned him to the past.

Rita's eye gleamed in accusation. In her stare he saw Rosario, his first wife, her ashen face framed in the window of her coffin. He saw little Justina, mute with grief, hobbling along with the funeral cortege. He saw Clemencia, his second wife, refusing Justina a place in their house. He saw Justina's stricken look when she learned that he'd allowed it.

Don Justo felt the pain of his past and he would not have it. No. He simply could not have it.

* * *

Much later don Justo awakened. A thin, exquisite pain flowered at his temples. He sat up and looked down at himself. He was still wearing his shirt and trousers and they were very crumpled. He was in bed, yet he had not removed his shoes. He could not tell what time it was. Soft light came through the window and he knew that he was home, but he could not recall coming here. He had been in the cantina. He remembered that now. He remembered the tequila burning a path down his throat. He tried to swallow, but his mouth was dry and he longed for a little water. He inched his legs over the edge of the bed, the movement a burden. He lifted a hand and watched it tremble. He'd done it up good. Ten years without a drop, and now he'd gone and done it.

Yoyo crawled out from under the bed and crept off toward the door. Don Justo looked around the room. In the corner, the bird cage stood uncovered. Its wire door was flung wide. Don Justo shuffled over to the birds. Romeo and Julieta huddled on the perch.

"¿Dónde está Rita?" don Justo said, little flashes of memory exploding in his head. A telegram. He had gotten a telegram. He dug into his pocket and pulled it out. Justina, he thought, stumbling to the chair. He remembered that too. Justina was gone and he would never have the chance to set things right with her.

Yoyo whined at the door. He looked over at don Justo and then at the door again.

A hollowness like a cave unfolded in his chest. There was something about the bed. The bed beckoned and he went to it. He flung aside the blanket and saw Rita's stiffened body.

Don Justo clapped a hand over his mouth, for he thought he might be sick. He fell upon the bed, gulping down the sourness in his throat.

After a time, he sat up and Yoyo came over and nudged him with his head.

"We'll be going to Guadalajara," don Justo said to the dog. He gathered up the bird, cradling its small body against his chest. "*Rita bonita,*" he said, and he did not turn away from the anguish breaking over him when he uttered her name.

Chapter 11

Esperanza Clemente

La Partera
(partera, n.f. midwife)

"Hijue puta," the woman grunted. She was propped up, half sitting on the birthing table and her legs were spread wide. Between them the head of her baby crowned, showing itself wet and dark and startlingly wondrous.

"Forget that and push," Esperanza Clemente ordered. She stood at the foot of the table, ready for the child. It was almost dawn, and she and the woman were in the part of Esperanza's house that served as her clinic. She had been a midwife and nurse for over twelve years. At each birth it was this moment that touched her the most.

"The man's a son of a whore," the woman said again, her face contorted in the stark light of the overhead bulb.

"Give one big push. One big one now." Esperanza cradled the emerging head, allowing it its smooth rotation until the profile of the child came into view. "It is almost done," she said, and the woman gave a sharp cry as Esperanza worked the baby's head until its shoulders appeared. Soon after, Esperanza said, "Look! You have another boy." The woman had four others at home. Esperanza held up this new, slippery one as though he was different from the rest. The woman fell back against the table, her face softened now, and glistening with perspiration.

Esperanza placed the baby on his mother's belly. She patted the woman's thigh. "You rest. You did good work." She said this at each delivery, and each time, she was awed and a little astonished at the part in it she played. She was thirty-five. She was alone in the world and childless, something not surprising for a defiled woman such as she was.

Esperanza cleared the baby's airway. She checked his color and stroked the pebbly path down his spine until he gasped and broke into a lusty bawl. "Listen to him."

The woman propped herself up on an elbow. She laid a hand on her son's moist head. "He sounds just like his father." She allowed herself a smile.

"Moments ago you were less complimentary."

"The man's a trial, no doubt of that." The woman collapsed against the pillows again.

Esperanza had heard it all before. "We all have our trials." She cut the cord and clamped it, and then cleaned the baby, whose dark hair stood up as if he had been frightened. She swaddled him in a blanket and placed him in the curve of his mother's arm. The woman offered the baby her breast, but he turned his face away, and so she poked a nipple into his tiny mouth. Soon he suckled her, a deep scowl lining his brow.

While the baby nursed, Esperanza kneaded the woman's belly to encourage the "second birth." When the placenta was delivered, she placed it in a jar for the woman to later bury in a place of her choosing. Esperanza soaked a cloth in an infusion of *cola de caballo* and *corteza de roble* that Remedios, the healer, had prepared for her. She sponged the woman off and provided a pad for her to wear. "You need to sleep." Esperanza motioned toward the freshly made cot against the wall.

"I have to go. I left the boys with him. It's almost morning." (This only two hours after the woman had knocked on Esperanza's door.)

"The man will be fine. The boys will be fine."

The woman laid her cheek against the top of her new son's head. He had stopped nursing and had dozed off. "You both need rest." Esperanza picked the baby up and placed him in the crib that was in the room. The woman climbed down from the table and reached for her clothes to slip them on, teetering a little as she did. "Maybe you're right," she said. "Maybe I'll lie down for just a minute or two."

Esperanza helped the woman to the cot. She drew a sheet around her and then snapped off the light and left the room. In the kitchen, Marta Rodríguez was making coffee. Since her aunt's death almost a year before, Marta had worked in Esperanza's house. The midwife was happy to have both her and her son. Marta was a quick and thorough worker. More than that, over the months she had become a friend.

"You're up early," Esperanza said. The wall clock near the sink read ten after five. She glanced out the window at the long, slender shadow cast by the papaya tree on the patio. Over the patio wall the sky was awash in color.

"Who could sleep with all that yelling." Marta poured a cup for herself and one for Esperanza. "Even Richard woke up, but I got him back to sleep." The boy was two years old now. Esperanza had been happy she could provide an opportunity for Marta to attend to her son.

Esperanza took the coffee Marta offered. "As I

remember, you did a lot of yelling yourself when Richard was born."

"And who could blame me? I was a baby myself. That woman in there is old." Marta blew into her cup, then took a sip. "What did she have?"

"Another boy. That makes five." Esperanza thought how the woman she'd just delivered was younger than herself, yet Marta believed her to be old.

Marta rolled her eyes as if just the thought of all those children was an effort in itself. She looked down at Esperanza's feet. "You should put on your shoes. You'll catch *la gripe*."

Esperanza laughed and wiggled her toes. The girl loved to give orders. "You sound like my mother."

Marta glanced away, two fingers hooked inside the neckline of her dress. "These days, I think a lot about my mother," she said.

"I know." The girl and she had much in common. Both had lost their mothers. Both were damaged women—ravaged, at an early age, in brutal, shameful acts.

A muffled knock came from beyond the kitchen, then a series of louder knocks followed.

Marta rolled her eyes again. "You're going to be busy today." She left, and soon she was back. "*Es el maestro*. He says it's his mother. It's her rheumatism again."

"Is Rafael still outside?"

"No. He left. He wants you to go over."

Esperanza sighed. She had been treating doña Lina for over two years. To put it mildly, the woman was very difficult.

"I'll get my shoes. While I'm gone, keep an ear out for the new one." Esperanza went down the hall and looked in on her patients before going into her room. At the dresser, she ran a comb through her hair and tried not to look too closely at the face staring back at her in the mirror. She was tired and looked it. Nevertheless, she rallied herself into a change of dress and put on her shoes. After grabbing her treatment bag, she hurried from the house.

At doña Lina's, Rafael opened the door. He was not a tall man, yet the set of his shoulders made him appear taller than he was. "It's been a bad night," he said. His trousers and shirt looked slept in. He closed the door and led her to his mother's room. Esperanza went in alone.

The room lay in shadows. In a corner, a small altar glittered with candlelight under a framed portrait of the Virgin of Guadalupe. Vases of paper flowers and antique statues of saints also rested on the altar. The room was filled with the cloying odor of burning candles and a night in which little sleep had come.

Doña Lina gave a cry when Esperanza came in. "*Ay, hija,*" she said, "*me estoy muriendo.*" Her great bulk was sprawled on a couch under the window that looked out onto the veranda. A coverlet was thrown over her so that only the top of her nightgown showed.

"No, no. You're not dying." Esperanza went to doña Lina's side, noting the aspirin bottle on the table next to the couch. A glass and a carafe sat on the table too. "I see you're taking your aspirin."

"Aspirin doesn't help," doña Lina said, her voice sliding into a whimper. "My knees hurt. So do my shoulders and hands." She lifted her hands and gestured stiffly. "My hands hurt the most."

"When was the last time you had aspirin?"

Doña Lina gave a helpless little shrug. "Last night sometime. Rafael gave it to me." She laid her head against the back of the couch. "That boy of mine. He wants to get rid of me."

"Come now. Why say such a thing?" In the past year, Esperanza had heard this talk before from doña

Lina. How Rafael was inattentive and self-centered. How he had changed from a good son to someone she could no longer count upon.

Doña Lina raised herself up. "It's true. Rafael planned a trip for me to Veracruz. My son Tomás and his family live there. Tomás has a big house. He has a cook and a servant just to watch the children."

"*Qué bueno.*" Esperanza shook four aspirins into her palm. She poured water from the carafe into the glass.

"I'm supposed to leave in ten days and stay a month, but I'm a sick woman. I think I shouldn't go." She drew her lips into a pout. "Rafael—he just wants to get rid of me."

The thought of Rafael alone, without his mother to tether him, flustered Esperanza. "Take these," Esperanza said, offering doña Lina the pills. "I'll bring warm compresses for your hands. Then it's time you got some sleep."

Doña Lina cleared her throat as though it were a reprimand. Reluctantly she took the pills and then allowed Esperanza to help her from the couch into the bed.

Rafael was on the veranda when Esperanza left the room. "How is she?" he asked.

"Your mother will be fine. I gave her aspirin." Esperanza started toward the kitchen at the far end of the veranda. "She needs some compresses." She called this out over her shoulder, hurrying away from the pull of Rafael's eyes, from the pull of his thinning hair and the little bald spot, like a tonsure, on the top of his head.

In the kitchen, Esperanza found two clean cloths. She went over to the sink and turned the tap on. When the water grew hot, she dropped the cloths in. She did not turn when she heard Rafael enter. Instead, she closed the tap and picked up the cloths. Gingerly, she squeezed hot water from them.

Rafael spoke up. "I planned a trip for her. To my brother's house in Veracruz."

Esperanza turned and caught him smoothing down his hair.

"Do you think she can go?" he asked.

"I don't know," Esperanza said. The moist cloths were in her hands, and the heat in them radiated up her arms, spreading toward her heart. She pictured Rafael freed for a time from his mother's petulance. She pictured a cleared path between her house and Rafael's.

"The trip, I think it will be good for her." He paused. "I think it will be good for me." He dropped his voice when he said this last, but held her gaze as if to lure her toward this conspiracy. "Good for you *and* me."

She made no response, for there was nothing she could say. He did not know the truth about her life. That she was a woman both defiled and undeserving. That because of it, she had never risked an involvement of the heart. Still, for some time, invisible currents had passed between herself and Rafael, and the thought of this sent a rush of heat to her forehead and cheeks.

"So, do you think she can go?" he asked.

"Only time will tell," she said, deciding in an instant to allow fate the lead. If she and Rafael were meant for each other, fate would show the signs. A sure sign would be doña Lina on a train heading out of town.

*   *   *

In the days that followed Esperanza went to doña Lina's house to treat her, usually just after lunchtime. Rafael was always there, and it was as if he had surmised her bargain with fate and given fate a boost himself: each day the swelling in his mother's hands lessened, thanks, in part, to his diligence in getting her to take around the clock the large doses of aspirin Esperanza had prescribed.

Esperanza took this as the first positive sign, and she began to allow Rafael's charged glances to soften her. She allowed herself to hope that despite all she had endured, she might now be worthy of another person's love.

On the fifth day, however, fate turned things in a new direction. When she arrived at the house, Rafael met her at the door. "She's sick again," he said, his eyes wild with apprehension. "She says she's in pain. I think her hands are swelling up again." Esperanza hurried inside.

Doña Lina was on the veranda. The radio novel she listened to each day had just ended, and she let out a wail when she saw Esperanza, saying she felt weak, because it was so hot and because Laura Esteban, the protagonist in the show, had learned she had cancer. To doña Lina, having cancer was the worst news you could get.

Doña Lina raised her hands and examined them in the broiling light of the afternoon. "Can you get cancer from rheumatism?" she asked.

"No, you can't get cancer from rheumatism," Esperanza replied, seeing at a glance that doña Lina's hands were not swollen but that she was in a state nonetheless, and it was this fact alone that could jeopardize all hopes. Esperanza saw another sign in this. *Ya ves*, fate was saying. You see. You really don't deserve a chance at happiness.

"Just the same, I'm going to die," doña Lina sniffled. She sank deeper into the easy chair.

Rafael stepped forward. "No, Mamá, you are not going to die." His voice was strong and there was a sudden sternness in it that was surprising. "Esperanza," he said, "can't you do something more."

"Well, there are infusions . . ." she said, letting her

voice trail off because it occurred to her that once again fate had shown its will. She would go to Remedios, consult with her on a remedy for doña Lina's hysteria.

"*Muy bien,*" Rafael said, "let's get what's needed." And because it was a directive and clearly something meant to be, Esperanza excused herself and left the house and climbed the hill to Remedios's hut.

It was a tea made from orange and magnolia blossoms, *tumbavaquero,* and *flor de tilia* that Remedios suggested for doña Lina's hysterics. For her rheumatic joints she recommended warm compresses soaked in sweet basil, arnica blossoms and the leaves of the ash tree. Esperanza brought the aromatics down from the hill and prepared the first round of them for Rafael in doña Lina's kitchen. After that it's up to him, she thought. Up to him and fate. She, of course, came by each day to check on her patient.

"Guess what. Tomorrow I'll be leaving," doña Lina said first thing when Esperanza arrived on the tenth day. As usual, Rafael had let her in and stood behind her now and she was grateful that he could not see the look of excitement that surely must have crossed her face. Doña Lina was spraddled in her easy chair. "It's too hot today," she said, wiping perspiration from her upper lip. She jutted her chin toward the bulky fan on the floor that nudged the sultriness around the legs of the furniture. "I need more air." She picked at the part of her dress that clung to the shelf of her chest.

"I can move the fan." Esperanza went over and unplugged it. "Where would you like it?" Out of the corner of her eye she noted that Rafael had gone to sit under the mango tree. He appeared engrossed in the newspaper.

"Over there. On the table."

Esperanza hoisted the fan from the floor. She plugged it in again. Soon a gale swept over doña Lina.

"It's too fast! My dress is riding up!"

Esperanza switched the speed lever to medium. She smoothed doña Lina's dress over her plump knees and down toward the black felt slippers she liked to wear. "There," Esperanza said. The woman was a cross, and once again Esperanza could clearly see the trial of Rafael's life.

Chac strolled up, his tail a black mast behind him. He jumped up on the wide sea of his mistress's lap, but she threw the cat off before he had a chance to settle himself. She lowered her voice to Esperanza. "My poor son. Tomorrow he'll be alone with only Chac for company." Doña Lina glanced out into the patio.

"You mustn't worry about Rafael. Concentrate on yourself. On how good it will feel to be on vacation."

Doña Lina's face lit up and for a moment Esperanza saw beyond the woman's egoism. She saw the need that mothered it, and she asked herself, what kind of misery might doña Lina have experienced to turn her vision so entirely upon herself.

"I trust you'll take care of yourself in Veracruz," Esperanza said.

"My son Tomás, he's hiring a nurse just for me." There was more than a touch of smugness in doña Lina's voice.

"How nice for you," Esperanza said. How nice for Rafael, she thought. Lest she spoil it, she did not extend the thought to include herself, though clearly this was a blessing cast in her direction.

Rafael stepped up onto the veranda, his newspaper tucked neatly under his arm. "Are you leaving? Let me walk you out."

"Well, yes," Esperanza said. She gave doña Lina a squeeze. "I'll see you in a month," she said, going off with Rafael. She did not look back, though she felt the weight of doña Lina's gaze on them all the way to the door.

The following evening, just after seven, Esperanza opened the door to Rafael. "*Hola,*" he said. He wore his hat, and his face lay in the shadow of its brim. "Mamá finally left," he said, poking his hands into his trouser pockets, as if with that gesture he'd put the thought of his mother away. That he was here was not entirely surprising, still Esperanza had spent most of the day pushing away the ridiculous thought that during the night doña Lina's hands had swollen into something so grotesquely large and misshapen that she had not been able to get them through the door of the train.

"Would you like some coffee?" Rafael asked. "We could go down the street and have a cup." He pointed down the sidewalk and then angled his face in such a way that it was now clearly visible. There was a look of expectation in his eyes, and his brow was furrowed as though preparing to try persuasion if she happened to decline.

She smiled. "Let me tell Marta." She left him at the door and went down the hall and into her room. At the dresser, she looked in the mirror and applied fresh lipstick. There was the same look in her own eyes that she had seen in Rafael's. On the way out, she stuck her head in the kitchen. Marta was at the table, feeding Richard. "I'm going out to the café."

"And may I ask with whom?" Marta said, widening her eyes to appear innocent.

"You may not," Esperanza said.

"You don't have to tell," Marta said. "You're going with *el maestro.*" She wiggled her eyebrows and giggled and Richard looked at his mother and giggled too.

"You're both impossible," Esperanza said and laughed. She joined Rafael and they started down the street.

It was a hot night in late January. The air was

humid and ripe with the smell of salt and fish, something that came with living so near the sea. Long-winged insects made dark halos around the street lamps. As though lacking the energy to complete the trip, a dog was stretched out in the middle of the street. People had dragged chairs into doorways, and they sat looking out, some moving the air with pleated paper fans. Others became mere shadows that sat in darkened rooms behind opened, barred windows. A few windows still sported faded swags and Christmas bells. As the couple passed by, people called out greetings, and Esperanza answered with a greeting of her own. Rafael merely raised a hand to his hat brim in response.

The café was air-conditioned and it had a large window that faced the street. There were cozy round tables with gray marble tops, and chairs with wire backs shaped like hearts. At the rear, a long glass case held breads and pastries. Along the wall there was an espresso maker with a maze of shiny tubes. Though the café was crowded, they found a table near the counter. When the waitress came up, they each ordered a cappuccino and pointed to the tray of *orejas* in the case.

"Well, here we are," Rafael said, after they'd settled themselves. He took off his hat and placed it on an empty chair. Soon the waitress came up and set down their orders. When she went off again, Rafael scooted his cup and saucer closer to himself. He had on a shirt the same hazel color as his eyes. Esperanza noticed this in the light of the café. She noticed, too, the full turn of his arms, the way his hand lay in a graceful curve around his coffee cup.

He looked across the table at her. "For the first time in a very long time, I am a happy man."

"Oh," Esperanza said and she looked down at her hands because something eased and bloomed inside her. She felt her face go warm.

"Did I speak out of turn?"

"Oh, no," Esperanza said, looking up at him again. "It's just that I'm happy too."

And so for a time they continued to be happy. He because he felt freed, he said. Because he felt roused from an endless, tortured sleep. She because the sight of him gladdened her and caused her pulse to quicken. Because with him fate was allowing her this chance.

Doña Lina had been away two weeks when Esperanza and Rafael went to dinner on the beach. Until that time they had shared frequent meals together, but these had been at Esperanza's house, or at various places in Santiago. Tonight they had gone to don Gustavo del Norte's restaurant, a roomy, airy place with an enormous thatched roof and rush walls and a magnificent view of the sea. It was a Friday night and the restaurant was gay with the noise of people enjoying themselves. Three guitarists strolled among the tables. Esperanza and Rafael finished their meal and, after paying the bill went down a flight of steps to the grassy promenade fronting the sea. The beach was bright with moonlight and the light coming from the restaurant made its own cheery glow. Other couples strolled about, and at the edge of the lawn, before the sandy slope that led onto the beach, a hammock maker, his shoulders stacked with merchandise, spread a sample of his work against the grass.

"Let's take a walk," Rafael said. He took Esperanza's hand as they ambled down the promenade, away from people, away from the lights and from the lilting sound of guitars.

They had gone a ways when Esperanza stopped. Impetuously, she slipped off her shoes and poked them into the ample pockets of her dress. "Let's go down to the water," she said. She hurried down the slope toward a calm sea, toward the shimmering path the moon laid along its surface. As she ran, she felt the heat of the day still trapped in the sand. Beside the shore, she allowed a wave to wash over her feet, and she laughed, because the water was cool and because she felt like a girl again. She turned and looked back at Rafael standing yet on the promenade. "Come," she yelled, and made motions to him, and he came lumbering down the slope because he was a formal man who would not take off his shoes.

They sat on a driftwood log that had washed up, away from the water's edge. They held hands, their fingers entwined, and she looked out across the water, at the low mountains across the bay that appeared as slumbering beasts in the distance. Atop one of the mountains, a beacon flashed, and it was like a star winking in her direction. "Look how beautiful," she said.

"It is you who are beautiful," Rafael said, and Esperanza turned to him. He pulled her close and cupped his hands around her face and kissed her.

His mouth was as sweet as it had been on those few times before when they had kissed, but tonight his lips were warmer and she felt a tremor go through him. She parted her lips to him like she had not done before. "*Mi amor*," he said, speaking the words against her mouth. He lifted his lips to her eyelids, and then he kissed her mouth again. "Rafa," she whispered and she threw her head back and he kissed the hollow of her neck and then he spread a hand over the fullness of her breast.

"Rafa," she said again, laying a hand over his, pleasure like a liquid rushing through her veins to warm her. But then a thought assailed her: A ravaged woman should not feel such happiness. In an instant, the thought cooled her. She brushed Rafael's hand away.

"What did I do?" he said, and then, "I'm sorry. I truly am. I didn't mean to hurt you."

"No, no. It's not that." She slipped off the log so that she was sitting on the sand. She pulled her legs close to her and embraced them. Years later, when she recalled this moment, she could not say what it was that unlocked her. Perhaps it was the wine they'd had at dinner, perhaps it was simply that, in the end, she knew fate was urging her toward a final test. Fate had flung a door wide open and now she must walk through it. She must tell him the truth about herself. How could they ultimately come together if there was no honesty to bind them first?

"Rafael," she said, "there is something you should know." She did not look his way when she spoke, but out across the sea, at the mountains and the twinkling beacon.

"What is it?" He had dropped down beside her and she felt his shoulder pressing against hers.

"Something happened when I was seventeen."

He was silent after she said this, and she could not tell if it was because he wished her to continue or wanted her to stop. Still she went on. "When I was seventeen my mother was still alive. She was a seamstress and sewed for rich families." She had not thought of her mother's work for a very long time. She had not thought about how the waiting room in her clinic had once been her mother's sewing room. There had been shelves in the room that had held bolts of fabric and spools of thread and stiff cards wrapped with ribbon and rickrack.

"Your mother. You lost her when you were seventeen." Rafael wrapped an arm around her shoulder and pulled her close.

"No," Esperanza said. "It's not that." She leaned into him, because she needed his nearness to go on.

"The year I was seventeen my mother was sewing

for a very rich family who had a grandmother living with them. *La abuela* was old and frail and she needed a nurse to care for her. That year, when the family was planning their annual trip to Miami, the nurse fell ill and could not make the trip. Mamá caught wind of this and spoke up. She had a daughter, she said, who had been to school and was serious about nursing. Before long it was arranged that I would take the nurse's place." Esperanza was silent, remembering how overjoyed she had been to be traveling out of Mexico. She'd had a boyfriend then, and they were engaged to be married, and he was not pleased to learn that she was going off like that.

Rafael squeezed her shoulder. "And then?"

She leaned her head against him and went on. "Miami was bright lights and tall buildings. The very air smelled different. The family's apartment was large, but my room was just a passageway between the kitchen and the back door where a cot and a dresser had been placed." She had hated the meagerness of this, the lack of privacy it presented, but she did not tell Rafael this, choosing instead to tell him about the patio where she'd sit with the grandmother in the shade of an umbrella. "*La abuela* was in a wheelchair, and each day I would wheel her around the turquoise water of the pool and along the row of palms edged along the patio."

Esperanza dropped her head onto her knees, feeling Rafael's shoulder next to hers, feeling the weight of his silence. In spite of it, she lifted her head and continued, to those late Miami afternoons, when the women shopped and *la abuela* dozed, and it was herself in the passageway and the man of the house coming toward her, and it was the cot and the man, a grunting beast who pinned her to it.

Esperanza dug her nails into her palms, remembrance flooding over her. After those times, she would steal into *la abuela*'s room. She would look at her lying still as a stone in bed, and *la abuela* would look up and silently study her. The old woman knew. She knew as surely as if she herself had been standing in the passageway. The smell of the man was in the air, and an outcry from her was all Esperanza would have needed to be rescued. But *la abuela* did not speak and Esperanza could not. How could she speak when speaking up would have brought the whole world down upon her?

"He said this, Rafael: He said that if I spoke he would call for the authorities. 'Certain authorities,' he called them. 'There are certain authorities working in this country,' he said. 'If you tell, I'll call for them and they will not believe you. In this country, they lock away whores like you.'"

Esperanza stopped speaking, for Rafael's shoulder no longer touched hers. She fought the urge to face him, to beg for his forgiveness as if it were she who had somehow been at fault. She looked down, at the rounded tips of his shoes that were two shadows stamped against the sand. "I was away two weeks. When I returned I told no one what had happened." Because she was ashamed, she could not tell her mother. She broke off her engagement. Would not talk to her boyfriend when he came by time and again, demanding explanations. After some months, he simply stayed away.

Esperanza risked a look at Rafael. He was staring off across the sand, his profile a sharp crag against the darkness beyond him. "Rafa," she said, her voice barely above a whisper.

"Who did this to you?" he asked, continuing to stare off.

"What does it matter. Long ago, the family moved away. I don't know where they are. I don't want to know."

He said nothing and he did not turn to look at her. After a time, he stood and brushed the back of his trousers with his hand. "We need to go," he said. He started off down the beach, in the direction of the restaurant. Esperanza watched him go, a numbness spreading over her like that numbness she'd felt when she'd come back from Miami and for a long time after.

*   *   *

A few days later, Esperanza Clemente was at her desk next to the window in the front room. It was Sunday afternoon, and the house was quiet. Marta and Richard were in the patio. Esperanza was going over the accounts she kept in the ledger with the pages edged in red. Periodically, she looked up from the ledger and gazed out the window. She tried not to think of Rafael. Tried not to think how that night, when he'd brought her home, he'd said the most perfunctory things, acting as if she'd laid an ocean between them and there were no boats to cross it.

As if the sidewalk had spit him up, Candelario Marroquín materialized at the window. He was inches away, his hands tight around two of the bars spanning the window.

"Esperanza," he said. "You must come to the house." He disappeared from the window, and for a moment, Esperanza thought he'd been a ghost, so quickly had he come and gone. She stood and looked out, and now he was pounding at her door. Esperanza hurried from the desk, running into Marta and Richard coming down the hall. Esperanza flung the door wide.

"It's Tonito," Candelario gasped. "He's dying." Tonito was Candelario's son. Two years before, Esperanza herself had delivered him.

"Where is he? What happened?" Esperanza asked.

Candelario laid a hand over his chest as if to try to catch his breath. "He's at the house. He was playing in the yard when he got sick. Chayo is with him. You have to come."

Esperanza turned around and Marta was slumped against the wall. "*Virgen santísima,*" she said, and Esperanza saw in the girl's face the specter of the spell that she'd had placed on Chayo's son before he was born. Esperanza wished she could stop and put her arm around Marta, offer her some comfort, but there was no time for that. She ran down the hall and fetched her treatment bag, and then she and Candelario rushed away.

A knot of neighbors were gathered in Chayo's yard. One woman gave a cry when she caught sight of the nurse. Esperanza hurried inside. Tonito was sprawled on the big bed in the corner. Chayo was at his side but Esperanza gently pushed her away. She bent over the boy and examined him. Tonito's body was grossly swollen. Esperanza took his pulse. His heart galloped. His mouth hung open, taking quick intakes of air, his exhalations wheezy. "Did something bite him?" she asked. "Was he stung?"

"He was playing near the anthill," Chayo said. She pointed feebly out the door.

Candelario stepped forward. "He likes to tease the fire ants. A couple of times before, the ants have bitten him."

Esperanza lost no time. The boy was in anaphylactic shock. "Find a car," she said to Candelario who looked in need of something to do. "We have to get him to the hospital."

Esperanza opened her bag to the sting kit she always carried. She took out a Syrette of adrenaline and injected the boy's arm, vigorously massaging the area around the injection site to speed diffusion. She propped him up and forced a dose of antihistamine down his throat. Because of the swelling, she feared his windpipe might constrict. If it did, a tracheotomy would have to be done.

Candelario ran in. "Santos was home. He'll take us in his taxi." He scooped his son up, and they all rushed out, the neighbors forming a path to the green Ford with sharp fins idling in the arroyo. Candelario laid his boy across the back seat, and Chayo, who had turned large after Tonito's birth, wedged herself in beside him.

Santos revved up the car as Esperanza and Candelario got in the front. As they took off, Esperanza glanced out the window and there was Marta standing under the lime tree, her son clinging to her. Going past, Esperanza raised a hand to Marta, but Marta did not wave back. Instead, she threw an arm around Richard as if to anchor him more securely to herself.

The car went bumping down the riverbed and soon they were on the highway and then in Manzanillo and at the hospital door marked URGENCIAS. Esperanza whisked the boy in through the double doors at the end of a hallway. She laid Tonito down on the table in one of the examining rooms. "*Tiene shok anafiláctico,*" she said and the doctors and nurses closed in around the boy and with that it was out of Esperanza's hands.

* * *

The sun had set when Esperanza reached home again. She let herself in and went to the kitchen and switched on the light. At the stove, she turned the flame on under the coffee. She was about to pour a cup when Marta walked in from her room. She looked wan and diminished. "Tonito died, didn't he?"

Esperanza went to her and placed an arm around her as if it were a wing for Marta to settle under. "Tonito didn't die. He's still in the hospital, but he'll be fine."

Marta dropped her head on Esperanza's shoulder and began to weep. The two held each other close for a moment, and then Esperanza led the girl to the table and sat her down. "Where's Richard?" Esperanza asked. She poured two cups of coffee and sat down herself.

"He's asleep. The commotion at Chayo's house upset him."

Esperanza took a sip of coffee. It was old and bitter. She set the cup down.

"I thought it was the end," Marta said. "I saw Tonito and I thought that he would die."

"Tonito's a strong boy," Esperanza said. "After he leaves the hospital, he'll be good as new."

"And Chayo?" Marta asked.

"She's fine. She's relieved, of course." Esperanza wished there was something she could do to mend the rift between Marta and her sister. A year or so ago, Esperanza had offered herself as a bridge between the two, but Chayo would have no part in crossing over.

"I know what Chayo thinks," Marta said. "She thinks Remedios never broke *el brujo*'s spell. She thinks it existed in some kind of suspension. That the spell was lying quiet until today." Marta shook her head.

Esperanza said nothing because what the girl said was true. At the hospital, while the doctors worked on Tonito, Chayo had walked round and round the waiting room, ranting about *el brujo* and how it was her sister who had brought this on her son.

Marta leaned across the table in demand of an answer. "It's true, isn't it?"

"*Sí*," Esperanza said, "*es verdad.*"

Marta slumped back into the chair. After a moment, she said, "Well, I thought the same thing too. Despite Remedios's efforts, for almost three years I have been waiting." Richard called out and Marta went toward the door. She paused when she came to it. "But thank God the wait is over. This scare today has broken *el brujo*'s spell. Maybe, with time, Chayo can forgive me." Richard called out again, a sleepy, whimpering voice, and Marta hurried toward it.

Alone once more, Esperanza stared at the table without seeing it. She thought how she would have to tell Marta that Tonito was still in danger. How this episode today was only the beginning of an ever-constant vigil. From today forward a single ant bite or bee sting could be lethal to the boy. The doctor and Esperanza herself had impressed this upon Chayo and Candelario. Chayo had wailed when she heard the perils lying before her son. She wailed at the fate that had given her Marta for a sister.

When Esperanza picked up her coffee, it had grown cold. She poured the coffee down the drain. She was rinsing the cup when a knock sounded at the door.

Going down the hall, Esperanza's heart was in her throat. Had Tonito's condition taken a turn? she asked herself.

It was Rafael at the door. He had taken off his hat and he clutched it in his hand. There was an expression of both sadness and misgiving in his face. Esperanza took a step back.

"Wait, don't turn away," Rafael said, lifting a hand to stop her. He dropped the hand at his side. "I'm sorry," he said, poking his chin into his chest. She could see the little bald spot at the center of his head.

Rafael looked at her, the street lights shining behind him. Still she saw into his eyes and there was regret in them. "The other night . . ." he said. "The way I treated you. It was wrong and I am sorry for it."

She was about to respond when he stepped up from the sidewalk and into the hall next to her. "Esperanza, listen to me. I am a foolish man and I made a mistake. I ask you to forgive me." He raised his hat to his chest and held it there as if to shield himself from rebuff.

She considered for an instant the earnest way he

stood before her and then she said, "Would you like some coffee? I was about to make some." She did not wait for him to answer, but turned and started down the hall toward the kitchen. She heard the door close behind her, but she did not look back to see if he was coming because she was certain he was there.

Chapter 12

Remedios Elementales: Aire

(aire, n.m. air)

Usually there is a breeze up on the hill where Remedios lives. Most times the breeze is gentle. It can carry the saltiness of the sea or the sharp sweetness of lemon groves or the loamy fragrance of newly worked earth. At times the breeze turns stiff and then it bears little aroma. When the wind is gusty, it moans around the bend of Remedios's hut.

Tonight it is mild and is murmuring a lullaby. Remedios lies on her cot under the opened window that looks out to the north. A waxing moon paints an arc beyond the crest of one *nogal*. The sky is splashed with stars and Remedios studies them. Before going to bed, she lighted the sweetgrass braid hanging from the top of the window frame, and its incense blessed and cleared her mind. Now, she closes her eyes and soon is swirling in a spiraled dream that lifts her up and toward the stars.

She is not alone on the journey. Her guardian, San Rafael Arcángel, accompanies her. He carries a staff, and together they stroll through mists as lofty as the angel's great vaulted wings.

Urraca is also with her, and bat, *murciélago,* because he is the totem for the ritualistic death all true healers must endure. Dragonfly wings along too. He guides her through illusions that cloud the never-ending road of transformation. Such loyal companions guide her to the center of the wind, to the place where the ancestors, the stars, reside.

Los antepasados, the ancestors, collect the wisdom of the Universe. *Los antepasados* burn bright with stored memory; they glow with stories. "*Siempre recuerda.* Always remember," the ancestors urge. Remedios remembers herself as she strides among the stars: how as a girl she walked both woods and shore and was awakened by the elements; how as a young woman the elements nurtured her. She remembers the old woman she now is and how the elements sustain her. *Soy la que sabe,* she thinks. Because I remember, I am she who knows.

After time among the stars, Remedios's spirit is rekindled. Guardian and guides return her to the cot. Remedios sleeps till sunrise. She has passed story back through her heart, where nothing dies away because it is remembered.

Chapter 13

Rosario "Chayo" Rodríguez de Marroquín

La Ramilletera
(ramilletera, n.f. flower girl)

It was midafternoon on Santiago beach when the wind started up, bringing with it the smell of rain. Tourists, what few there were of them—it was August and the rainy season—collected towels and canvas bags and went lurching across the sand toward the chalky hotel looming like a rampart along the shore. Some were not so quick to leave. They stood, their backs to the hotel, hands aligned over brows, looking up from sea to sky as if between the two existed a conspiracy. Chayo Marroquín lost no time. She plucked up her flower basket and hurried over to a young couple lingering behind. She had approached the pair a few hours earlier, and the man had looked up from a book, then away, before returning to the book again. The woman, a very blond and tan woman, had noticed the rebuff. She had smiled sweetly at Chayo, a narrowed eye on the man, but in the end, she waved Chayo away as if to say, if he won't buy for me, why do it for myself. Chayo

Marroquín was good at reading tourist's minds. In this business, where all day it was heat and sand and the fickleness of strangers, an ability like mind reading could make a lot of difference.

"¿*Florecitas de papel?*" Chayo addressed the man with the same words she always spoke, but this time she raised a bouquet of yellow poppies to the woman's face for comparison. "Pretty girl, pretty flowers," she said, selecting one of the useful English phrases she had memorized.

The woman took the small bouquet and cocked her head and giggled and batted her eyelids at the man until he laughed at her antics. "¿*Cuánto?*" he asked finally, and Chayo told him. He paid, and soon the pair went off across the beach, leaving little hollows in the sand to mark their passing.

Chayo pocketed the bills. She looked up at the darkening sky and up the beach in search of her son Tonito who had Chiclet packs to sell. On Saturdays she bought boxes of gum at the *tianguis,* the Indian market, marking up each pack for quick sale on the beach. Chayo spotted Tonito up near the hotel. To get his attention, she gave a sharp clap and pointed to the sky, twirling a finger in the air to indicate departure.

As the wind picked up, Chayo spread a plastic sheet over her flowers and tucked the edges in around the basket. She had sold only half of her bouquets today. In her pocket were perhaps ten thousand pesos. At home there was three times that amount, a sum that over the weeks she had managed to stash away for Esperanza Clemente's wedding which was fast approaching. There were expenses for the occasion: Chayo's dress and, because Tonito was in the wedding, a new white shirt for him and trousers, too. As a special gift to *la partera,* Chayo would make *mole* for the wedding feast. The ingredients of the dish were many and costly, but such was life. Besides, there was nothing Chayo would not do for Esperanza. The woman was a saint. Over a year ago, she had snatched Tonito from the very doors of death.

Chayo and Tonito made it to the road when it began to rain. Chayo spotted the shell of a small building sitting along the way. Don Justo, *el pajarero*, stood in the doorway, waiting out the weather. He motioned for them, stepping aside when they ran in.

"*Buenas, Don Justo*," Chayo said. "It's been some time since I've seen you." She and *el pajarero* frequently worked the same beach, so it did not surprise her to find him here. She set her basket down, giving it a little shake before she did. She looked around. The place was unfinished. The windows were not framed or glassed in. Construction debris was piled on the concrete floor. Don Justo's bird cage and his fortune-telling equipment were next to the door. Chayo went to stand beside him, and they both looked out toward the cobblestoned road that led down into town.

"It was slow today," Chayo said. She had to raise her voice when she spoke because of the sound of the rain.

Don Justo shrugged and spread his hands palms up. "It's the slow season." He was an old man who, since she'd seen him last, seemed to have shrunk. His clothing hung on him as though on the back of a door. Chayo looked around for his old yellow dog. When she did not see it, she asked, "*¿Y su perro?*"

Don Justo shrugged again. "*Se murió.*"

"Oh, I'm sorry," Chayo said. In the past, she had never seen him without his dog. Now she realized that he looked like he was missing a limb without the dog beside him. "How did he die?"

"He was old. He was as old as me."

Chayo nodded and said nothing.

"Yoyo was a good dog," he said.

Behind them there was a cry and Chayo turned to see Tonito take a spill on the dusty floor. He dropped his box of Chiclets. Chayo rushed over. She pulled him up by an arm. "You were running. Look at your Chiclets." Cellophaned packs of turquoise and pink gum were scattered about.

Chayo inspected him for damage. The boy whimpered and she brushed off his bottom and the back of his legs. "Hush, now. You're fine."

Don Justo came over. A blue canary rode on his finger. "Look. This is Carolina."

Tonito turned quiet. He watched don Justo raise the bird to his face and pucker his lips which had little wiry hairs sprouting at the corners. "*Dame un beso,*" don Justo said, and the bird pecked the old man's lips. He offered the bird for Tonito to kiss, but he backed away from it.

"Carolina won't peck you. She's a good bird."

Tonito held a finger out and don Justo put on a serious face for the boy. "Do you think you're big enough to hold Carolina?"

Tonito nodded. "I'm almost four." Don Justo knelt beside the boy, and while the rain came down, he allowed the bird to sit on the boy's shoulder and hop up and down his arms. Chayo watched this out of the corner of her eye as she picked up Chiclet packs. She lined them up in the box again, pleased to see that more than half the box was empty. She smiled. The boy had not done bad today.

The rain stopped as abruptly as it had begun. "*Vamos,*" don Justo said. He placed Carolina in the cage again, and the group gathered their things up. They stepped out into the freshness and bright smell of loam. Soon they were plodding down the twisting road, don Justo at the lead, his bird cage and equipment stacked high on his back. The three kept well to the side of the road and when they reached the bottom, don Justo crooked a finger at the boy. "Don't forget to have your mother read your fortune."

"What fortune?" Chayo said.

"I gave him a fortune." *El pajarero* waved and started toward town.

Chayo set down her flower basket. "Let me see."

Tonito handed over a slip of blue paper that he had trapped between his chest and gum box.

Chayo took the fortune and for an instant she considered reading it, but then she crumpled it up and threw it down. "These fortunes are absurd," she said. "I don't believe in things like that."

A bus rumbled by, shifting gears and spewing acrid smoke. Chayo jerked Tonito toward her. "Get away from the road," she said, though they both stood well back from it. "Haven't I told you the road is dangerous."

Tonito broke away from his mother. He bent over and reached for the little paper.

"Leave that where it is," Chayo said. She gave the boy a push to start them on their way.

* * *

Two days before Esperanza's wedding, Chayo started the *mole*. To make *mole* you need three kinds of chiles: *chiles anchos, mulatos* and *chiles pasilla.* You need onion and garlic, a handful of almonds and just as many sesame seeds. You need blanched peanuts and squares of bitter chocolate, as well as whole cinnamon and pepper, whole anise and clove. When Chayo made the sauce, something she did on only special occasions, she kept to the family recipe. Today, after Candelario had gone off to fish, she went to the market with Tonito. Now all the ingredients were spread on the table. On the stove sat a pot for the turkey, the vegetables and herbs. These would make the broth that would silken the sauce. Once prepared, Chayo would ladle the *mole* into the earthenware jar that Nacha, the finest potter in the market, had made on special order. The pot sat on the middle of the dresser, pushed back and away from the sides for safety's sake. It was a rich brown color and there was a trail of blue delphinium around the lip and vase. The names Esperanza and Rafael formed a band around the middle.

Before getting started, Chayo poked her head outside. "Tonito," she yelled. Last she looked, the boy had been at the makeshift coop his father had strung up next to the house. Tonito was there now, crouched beside the wire mesh, poking tufts of grass through an opening toward the turkey. "What are you doing?" Chayo said.

"You don't have to kill it. It could be my pet." Tonito jerked a finger away when the bird came near it.

Chayo shook her head. What had possessed her to tell the boy the turkey was for the wedding feast? "Turkeys are for eating. They're not for pets."

"I don't like to eat turkey."

"You like turkey. Come in now. Come inside with me." They started toward the door just as Santos, their neighbor, came out of his house. He walked over to the coop. "What is this?"

"I'm making *mole* for *la partera*'s wedding."

"My mother used to make *mole*," Santos said. He was a large man with a big belly and a small head. "Every Christmas she made it. She was from Oaxaca. There's good *mole* in Oaxaca."

Tonito tapped Santos on the leg. "She's going to kill the turkey."

"To make good *mole* you have to kill a turkey," Santos said. "My mother killed turkeys. She was very good at it. She laid their necks on a rock and chopped off their heads." Santos looked away as if peering into his past. "Yes, the blood really flew on the days Mamá made *mole*."

"Where's your taxi?" Chayo asked to change the subject. Santos could go on. He had impressed Tonito. The boy's mouth was hanging open. He glanced at the coop, then studied his mother.

Santos scratched his neck. "These days, I have to park it up the street. I can't drive down the arroyo." He hooked his thumbs in his waistband and went over a few meters to look at the riverbed. Chayo steered her son away from his preoccupations. They went to stand under the lime tree at the edge of the yard. "Look at that," Santos said, cocking his head toward the arroyo.

Up and down its length, the arroyo was a mud hole. A stench came from it that, when the wind was right, made living here difficult. Today there was hardly a breeze and that made life tolerable. "We should fill the arroyo up," Chayo said.

Santos threw his head back, pulling his fingers from his waistband. "*¡Ajá!* That's good! We fill it up, I drive my taxi to my door."

Chayo laughed too. "We should go down to the *ayuntamiento*. Demand that the governor fill the stinking thing up."

"That will be the day. *El gobernador* doing something for the people. Besides, he couldn't fill it up. The arroyo leads right out to sea." He leaned over and peered up the arroyo as if the ocean itself were only meters away.

Tonito tugged at Chayo's dress. He pointed at the turkey coop. "You won't chop off its head, will you, Mamá?"

Chayo lifted her son into her arms and hugged him. "This boy, all he talks about is turkeys. I better get to my *mole*." It was going on nine o'clock. If she didn't stop Santos, he would go on forever. Chayo set the boy down. She took leave of her neighbor, and she and Tonito went inside.

What she would do was flame the chiles, peel them and scoop out the seeds. She would toast the almonds and the sesame seeds in a very hot pan. She would grind the spices on the stone mortar that had been her mother's. This she would do, *then* she would kill the turkey.

There was a knock on the door and Tonito ran to open it. It was Marta with Richard at her side.

Chayo stepped around the table at which she had been standing. "You know you're not welcome here," she said. There was that look on her sister's face that begged for forgiveness. Chayo had seen it many times before and was hardened against it. What was done was done and no pleas from Marta would change what had come before.

Tonito hurried up to Richard. "You want to see my turkey?" He took his cousin's hand and pulled him out of sight.

"You better go too," Chayo said, making a quick motion of dismissal with her hand.

Marta stood her ground. "Listen to me. It's been four years. I've paid for what I did. I pay for it everyday."

"You can never pay enough."

Marta started to step inside, but Chayo stopped her with an upturned hand. At Chayo's request, Candelario had painted the walls of the room a bright blue, and Marta must not come in, lest she alter the field of protection the color blue offered.

Marta let her arms drop to her sides. "I'm your sister. Now that tía Fina's gone, Richard and I are your only living relatives."

"Richard is always welcome. But you, you might as well be dead."

Marta slumped against the door frame. "Why can't you forgive me?"

Marta's voice was so plaintive that for a moment it

touched Chayo, but then she thought of her son and how he had been cursed to a life of vigilance against bee stings and insect bites.

"Won't you ever forgive me?" Marta asked.

"For what you did, there is no forgiveness."

Marta stared at Chayo and after a moment, she said, "Were I in your place, I would never be as cruel."

"Don't be too sure," Chayo said as she strode over and closed the door.

*   *   *

Esperanza and *el maestro*'s wedding took place early on Saturday at La Iglesia del Carmen in Santiago. After the ceremony, a breakfast of *atole y tamales* was held at the bride's house, and in the evening, there was a dinner at the home of the groom's mother. From the start, the wedding plans had veered a little from tradition. For one, Esperanza herself had fixed the breakfast, not having living parents to do it for her. And when she walked down the aisle, it was not a wedding gown she wore, but a pale rose dress with a flared skirt and lace panels at the waist and neck. Contrary to custom, she had approached the groom unaccompanied. Standing in the pew, Chayo had poked an elbow into Candelario's arm, but she had said nothing, being that one had to make concessions for a bride who was not caught in the blush of youth. When Esperanza glided by, Chayo craned her neck and she looked toward the front of the church at doña Lina, *el maestro*'s mother, who stood in the first pew. Doña Lina was slumped against the arm of her oldest son, Tomás. After the wedding Tomás would take his mother home to live with him and his family in Veracruz.

Now, three hours into the wedding feast, Chayo sat under a mango tree growing in the patio of doña Lina's house. Chayo fanned herself with a hand. Bad weather threatened. In the afternoon it had rained, a hard driving rain typical for this season. People said how convenient it was the rain had come between the celebrations. They said a good rain freshened the air so that hairdos stayed up and dresses stayed crisp. But now the night had turned humid and clouds gathered overhead. Chayo was certain that, somewhere, people were taking bets on whether or not the rain would hold off until Esperanza and *el maestro* were safely on the midnight bus to Guadalajara.

Doña Lina's house was luminous. Tree branches spreading out above Chayo were studded with lights. There were lights wrapped around the columns of the veranda, which was crowded with guests, a large number of them *el maestro*'s students. The children had made a playground of the rooms of the house and Tonito and Richard were running in and out. Soon after dinner (there had been three roasted turkeys as well as Chayo's *mole*), Chayo had lost track of the boys. Since the party began the boys had been inseparable, each in black trousers and white shirts and so near in age they could have passed for twins. Earlier Tonito had asked Chayo if, after the party, Richard could come home with them. Chayo said she'd think it over. She had taken Richard into her house before, for it was not with him that she was feuding. But on those occasions it had been Esperanza who had brought the boy over and tonight Esperanza would not serve as the go-between. Tonight she was on the veranda dancing with *el maestro* to the chords of three guitarists hired for the occasion. Since the wedding, Esperanza had loosened her hair and changed into a traveling dress. Chayo watched the couple dance. They danced slowly, looking into each other's eyes and so close together they could have been one.

Doña Lina kept an eye on them too. She had

danced a dance with her son and then collapsed into a large upholstered chair. Now the chair seemed to be swallowing her up. Chayo shifted in her own seat, straight-backed and uncomfortable. She had eaten too much *mole* and now her dress was very tight in the waist. Fermina, the best seamstress in the market, had fashioned it from a length of violet fabric Chayo had bought at the *tianguis*. The way she felt, she wished she had not insisted on the set-in waistband, but had taken Fermina's suggestion of a dropped waist instead.

Luz Gamboa plunked herself into an empty chair next to Chayo. "¡*Ay!* my feet are killing me," she said. Luz had on a green dress featuring an off-the-shoulders neckline. Clusters of colored glass cascaded from her earlobes. Luz raised her foot a bit as if to examine her shoe. Her shoes were almost the same color as her dress. The leather on the front of the shoes was gathered into bows. "These are half a size too small," she said to Chayo. "The man didn't have my size, but I wanted them anyway. I just love these little bows."

Chayo laughed. What we women won't do, she thought. It was a wonder Luz could walk. She had danced in those shoes for more than an hour with César Burgos. Luz was a bright spirit in César's arms. Though he was a serious man, his eyes lighted up with Luz beside him. Beto, César's son, watched them as they danced, a smile playing on his lips. "You and César are starting to look serious," Chayo said.

Luz lowered her foot. "Oh, I don't know. César and I, we understand each other."

"That's always a good beginning," Chayo said.

"Yes. Maybe so."

Candelario came over and stood next to Chayo for there was not an empty chair left on the patio or here under the tree. Cande wore his good trousers, the ones with pleats at the waist that Chayo had to talk him into buying. "Tonito wants Richard to come home with us tonight," he said.

"Where are the boys?" Chayo picked demurely at the front of her dress, which had grown damp with perspiration.

Cande squatted down beside her, and Chayo caught a whiff of the lemony cologne she had bought for him at the *tianguis*. "They're inside, watching Fulgencio Llanos take pictures of the people."

Luz said, "César and Beto are having theirs taken. Not me. I don't like my picture taken."

"Ah," Chayo said. She looked past the veranda at the lighted windows that looked in on the rooms of the house. When Marta came out of the dining room and glanced into the patio, Chayo looked away. She had been lucky. At the church and at breakfast, and even during dinner, Marta had kept her distance.

Tonito and Richard came running up. They were both out of breath. "Look what *el fotógrafo* gave me," Tonito said. He puffed his chest out and handed a photograph to Chayo. It was one of those instant kind with the backing and the wide white border around the image. In the photograph Tonito stood very straight, his arms clapped at his sides. He wore a sober expression as if he were being scolded when the picture was taken.

"You're so serious here," Chayo said, giving a little tap to the photograph. She handed it to Cande for him to have a look.

"He gave me one too," Richard said, offering up his photograph.

Chayo laughed when she saw it. In the picture the boy's head was tilted to one side and his eyes were wide with expectation. The ends of his mouth were turned up. "*El fotógrafo* caught you smiling!" she said. That was something Richard did not often do.

Cande leaned over and took a look too.

"Can I come home with Tonito tonight?" Richard asked, knitting his brows to show how much he wanted it.

Chayo rumpled the boy's hair. "*Muy bien.*"

The boys gave a little jump of delight. "I'll tell my mother," Richard said and the two ran off.

Chayo gathered up the photographs and placed them in her pocket. "You arrange it," she said to Cande, glad she did not have to utter Marta's name.

* * *

The four of them ran to outdistance the rain. Doorlamps up and down the street cast coins of light along the sidewalk and the children bolted in and out of them, frisky as colts escaping a corral. Tonito yelled gleefully, dodging fat raindrops, while Richard ran with his face turned up, his mouth open to the rain. Halfway up the block, Chayo stopped to pull off her high heels. She was hooking a finger through the straps when Cande ran into her. "Uff!" Chayo said, and she laughed and steadied herself and gave him a push as though for revenge. Cande laughed too, and he reached out for her and pulled her close. For a moment they were like a couple doing a slow dance under the light of the corner street lamp.

Lightning penciled the sky, and soon after thunder rumbled. Richard slowed down and stuck his fingers in his ears. "You afraid of thunder?" Chayo said, running up to him. He nodded gravely and she handed her shoes to Cande, who was right behind her. "Your auntie has you now," she said, lifting the boy into her arms and hugging him tightly. "Let's hurry home."

They made it inside just as the sky collapsed. They stood at the window, the room dark around them, and looked out at the blur of rain and at the smudge of brightness the light at the door made along the edge of the house. The lime tree was a whipped-up shadow at the lip of the arroyo. The window fogged over and Cande made a fist and rubbed a circle in the glass. The boys giggled and did the same.

The arroyo'll fill up, Chayo thought. She pictured the river overflowing as it had years ago, when they had first come here to live. Back then the water had reached halfway up the yard before it started to recede. Now the rain was an interminable drumroll on the roof and she did not want to think about the storm and the muck and stench it could bring right to her door.

Chayo ran a hand over the skirt of her new violet dress. Her dress was damp, her hair too. She had to change. Dry her hair. The boys also needed her attention. In the darkness, she felt her way to the dresser, the soles of her feet stinging still from the run over concrete. She opened the side of the dresser that was a wardrobe and unzipped her dress. She was about to take it off when she remembered the photographs. She took them from her pocket and peered at them, but she could not make out the boys. She propped the photos against the dresser mirror, their white rims making two ghostly squares in the gloom.

Chayo changed and flipped on the light and took a towel to her hair. She dried the boys off as well. She found something of Tonito's for Richard to wear. Tonito would sleep in the big bed between his parents, Richard on Tonito's cot against the wall. The four settled down for the night, but Chayo could not sleep, her mind churning like the weather. She told herself they were safe inside the house, but the odor of the storm, a sweetish smell tinged with something foul, stole in under the door and around the edges of the windows and unsettled her. Chayo closed her eyes and tried to lull herself to sleep, but in her mind there was Esperanza and *el maestro* traveling over perilous highways toward Guadalajara. In her mind there was her sister riding out the storm alone in Esperanza's house. Chayo opened her eyes and gazed up into the darkness. Soon she made out her paper flowers hanging in bunches from the ceiling. The nearness of her flowers and the blueness of her walls was comforting.

After a time Chayo fell asleep, but she did not know it until she snapped awake. Someone was pounding on the door. Chayo pulled herself up and reached across Tonito to shake Cande's shoulder. He came awake with a jerk and then he, too, heard the pounding. He sprung out of bed and pulled on his trousers before going to the door. He opened it to Santos.

Chayo fell back against the pillow, realizing in a rush that it was Marta whom she'd expected at the door.

Santos yelled above the sound of the storm. "There's a pig in the arroyo."

Cande ran out and Chayo hurried over to the door. It was almost dawn. There was a greenish cast to the growing light outside. It amazed her to find the rain had ended. The rumble she was hearing was not the storm, but the arroyo. A froth of brown water churned down the riverbed, the water so high she could see it from the door. She went quickly to the dresser and changed out of her nightclothes, careful not to awaken the boys. Throughout the commotion the boys had slept and she was happy they were spared this. She let herself out, closing the door behind her.

She saw it the moment she stepped outside. The lime tree was gone. All that marked where it had stood was a black wound in the earth. Chayo glanced down the arroyo, and the tree was there, wedged between the riverbanks. Chayo ran toward the tree, toward Cande and Santos, the air so moist and heavy it was like a barrier to run through.

The pig was caught in the tree. It was a gray pig, a suckling pig by the size of it. Its front legs were caught at the point where they joined its chest in the V tree branches make. The pig's head was high and its eyes were wild. It squealed a continuous high scream that sliced through the sound of the rushing water.

The tree rocked with the force of the water, its roots a wormy claw rising and falling against the bank. "We'll free the pig and have a pig roast," Santos yelled. He grasped a tangle of roots and lowered himself into the river. The swiftness of the current swept him hard against the tree. He hooked an arm over a clump of branches and clung to them. If he had wanted, he could have touched the pig.

"I'll get a rope," Cande yelled. He ran toward the house and Chayo ran after, yelling at him that only fools risked their lives for a roasting pig. Cande ran back with a net and a rope and he quickly made a noose at one end of it. He threw the end to Santos, who poked his head through and then lowered it under his arms. Cande pulled the rope taut and handed it to Chayo. "Don't let go," he said.

Too surprised to argue, Chayo held on. Santos's wife came out of her house and she ran over and held on too. Other neighbors had come outside, but they were on the opposite bank and could do nothing but stand and watch.

Cande flung the net over the river and for a moment it was a turquoise circle before it landed on the pig. The pig grunted in surprise and then squealed again, its screams more piercing than before. Cande reclaimed the rope and played it out. Santos, because he was tethered, used the tree as a buttress and worked the net around the pig.

Santos threw his weight against the animal until it

slipped through the branches entrapping it. The pig sank like a boulder, Santos diving after it. "¡*Chinga!*" Cande cried. He dug his heels in and used the rope to haul Santos up and reel him in.

Santos helped pull himself up over the edge of the riverbank, his clothing plastered to him. He shook the water from his hair and stepped out of the rope that had encircled him.

"Look," Chayo said. She pointed to the pig trapped in the turquoise net shooting down the river, riding the crest of a foamy brown wave.

"There goes dinner," Santos yelled and they all laughed. Even the neighbors on the opposite side threw back their heads and laughed, though you could not hear them do it.

Chayo looked up the river toward home. It was much lighter now and she saw that the blue door of the house was standing open. She frowned because she was sure she had shut the door. It was then she saw Tonito. He had his back to her, but she recognized his T-shirt with the yellow Batman grin. Tonito stood over the gaping hole the lime tree left behind. Chayo yelled out to her son for he was much too close to the river bank.

A fierce hum of dread started up in Chayo's ears. She rushed toward her son when the soil under his feet gave way and he dropped into the hole.

Chayo screamed and sprang to the hole, peering down into it, but Tonito was gone. She thought some monstrous joke had been played on her when she heard Cande yell. Tonito was in the river. She could see the back of his head bobbing in the water. She could see his arms raised above him as if for balance.

It was the lime tree that stopped him.

Chayo bolted toward her son as the current spun him around. It was then she saw his face. It was not Tonito in the river, but Richard. Richard, her sister's son.

Cande took up the rope and pulled the noose end of it over his head, tightening it under his shoulders. He dropped into the river even before Santos picked up the other end of the rope to steady him.

Chayo was at the river's edge and was ready to plunge in herself when the lime tree groaned. Gracefully, because there is grace even in such things, the lime tree was unhinged. Like a green leafy gate opening, the top of the tree swung away from the riverbank. Richard moved with the tree, his little mouth opened in a noiseless scream. He lifted one arm toward his aunt and uncle before the river swept him away.

Chapter 14

Remedios

La Curandera
(curandera, n.f. healer)

Remedios squats at the edge of the sea, the swordfish beak, *el pico*, lying across her lap. All day she has been here. To the left, a stone's throw away, a promontory rises. On that side of the crag, the sea is rugged. But here the sea is coved and protected, and were there less rockiness and more beach, it might have been a place for tourists.

The sun is low. Waves bring sea foam a few meters from her feet, then gently chase it, but Remedios hardly notices. Her gaze is fixed on a point on the horizon. It is from there the boy's body will come. And he will come, here, to her. She had seen this, four years before, when the boy was only movement in his mother's womb. Back then the girl had come, a child herself, wild with regret over what she had done.

And *la curandera* had undone it.

Remedios had purified herself. She had drunk a potion of herbs and San Pedro cactus, and *Urraca*, her familiar, had come to her. Because the girl required it, the bird and Remedios's spirit had flown out across the sea and then back to land again. Fortified with the might that salted air bestows, they had hovered over *el brujo*'s house and called an *urra, urra,* expunging the sorcerer's spell. Remedios attested to this, as she could now attest that there were other things to tell about the girl.

Until an hour or so ago, the girl had been here, sitting next to Remedios, but now Marta was on the other side of the crag. Throughout the day, she had made frequent trips back and forth. Over there family and friends were collected, for it was their thought, Marta said, that a body returns to the very place where the sea claimed it.

Remedios knows differently, of course.

Some time later, Marta and her sister Chayo appear over the top of the crag. They take their time descending, making their way carefully over jagged rocks. Soon enough they are on the beach and sitting, side by side, next to Remedios.

"Cande is out there in his boat," Marta says.

"César Burgos is out in his," Chayo adds. "Everyone is waiting. Even Santos with his taxi."

The three are silent, for it is understood that it is in Santos's taxi that the body will be transported. The women scoot back away from the water and for a time watch the sea. Then Marta says, "This is the place where Roberto raped me." Her voice is flat when she speaks it.

"I know," Remedios says. It had happened back there where the sharp sea grass grew. Remedios had seen it in the vision she had when the girl had come for a *florecimiento,* the centering ritual that had been her final healing. It was then, too, that she had brought *el pico* back down to the sea. Plunging its end into the water, it had shown her what she was certain of today: seed spilled on this shore to this shore returns.

Marta says, "I keep asking myself, which wave is it that will bring me back my son."

"Each wave has its own reason," Remedios says.

"I will lose my mind when the right one comes."

"Yes, this is true," Remedios says, "but you won't be lost for long." She herself is ready to receive the little body. She has brought cloth to wrap him and a hammock in which to carry him. Sprigs of rosemary and laurel she has brought to sweeten him.

"When the boy comes in, he will not look like himself," Remedios says. She thinks, there will be bloat, the damage that feeding fish cause.

Chayo lowers her head and presses a fist to her mouth. She begins to sob softly. Marta lays an arm around her sister's shoulder and holds her close. After a time, Marta says, "When this is over, I will take the bus to El Paso."

Chayo raises her head with a start. "No, Tita," she cries.

Remedios merely nods. The sun is a fiery disk sinking into the horizon.

Remedios stands, sinking *el pico* deep into the sand. "The boy nears," she says, catching in the flash of the setting sun the phosphorescent green of *Urraca* wings.

Glossary of Spanish Words and Phrases

Section 1: Chapters 1–5

¿A qué venís?: Why have you come?   *p. 57*
Andale: Go ahead.   *p. 36*
aquí: here   *p. 29*
¡Basta!: Enough!   *p. 19*
cal: lime (calcium hydroxide)   *p. 22*
comedor: restaurant   *p. 25*
cómo exagera: how you exaggerate   *p. 25–26*
Dame las manos: Give me your hands.   *p. 53*
el agua del desencanto: water of disenchantment   *p. 44*
el cura: the priest   *p. 10*
el pico de pez espada: the beak of the swordfish   *p. 3*
Es cierto: It is true.   *p. 53*
¿Estás bien?: Are you all right?   *p. 44*
¡Fuera!: Get out!   *p. 37*
¡Híjole!: Good God!   *p. 43*
indio de la chingada: Indian screwup   *p. 20*
la mesa santa: the sacred table; altar   *p. 3*
la tortillera: the tortilla maker   *p. 46*
Madre de Dios: Mother of God   *p. 38*
mercado: market   *p. 30*
mesón: rooming house   *p. 48*
Mi carro es muy grande: My car is very big.   *p. 29*
Mira, es Juan Travolta: Look, it's John Travolta.   *p. 50*
mis machetes: my machetes   *p. 37*
nada: nothing   *p. 37*

No, creo que no: No, I don't think so. *p. 31*

nogales: walnut trees *p. 21*

paciencia: patience *p. 33*

patrón: owner *p. 6*

¿Qué pasa?: What's going on? *p. 32*

¿Qué pasa aquí?: What's going on here? *p. 37*

¿Qué pasó? ¿Qué fue?: What's happened? What is it?
  p. 48

¿Quién es?: Who is it? *p. 39*

¿Quién sabe?: Who knows? *p. 51*

¿Quién sos?: Who's there? *p. 57*

Sí, muy malo: Yes, very bad. *p. 33*

Soy la que sabe: I am she who knows. *p. 23*

Toma: Take these. *p. 44*

Vamos: Let's go. *p. 35*

vigas: beams *p. 21*

violación: rape *p. 16*

Yo soy el ensaladero: I am the salad maker. *p. 11*

Section 2: Chapter 6–8

Ay, hombre, tomar un taxi es muy caro: Ah, friend,
  taking a taxi is very expensive. *p. 93*

barranca: ravine, gorge *p. 94*

buenas tardes: good afternoon *p. 63*

comal: a clay pan used for baking tortillas *p. 60*

¿Cuántos años tiene?: How old is she? *p. 67*

Entren: Come in. *p. 92*

Es hora de mi novela: It's time for my story. *p. 68*

La indita es muy buena: The Indian girl is very good.
  p. 67

la muchacha: the girl *p. 67*

La verdad, mi vida es una pura mierda: It's true, my life
  is a complete mess. *p. 94*

Nada. Absolutamente nada: Nothing. Absolutely nothing. *p. 88*

Soy alma, soy espíritu: I am soul, I am spirit. *p. 60*

Soy fuego: I am fire. *p. 60*

Soy luz: I am light. *p. 60*

tianguis: market *p. 73*

un amate: a fig tree *p. 61*

Yo tuve la culpa: I was to blame. *p. 96*

Section 3: Chapters 9–11

Ay, hija, me estoy muriendo: Ah, dear, I am dying. *p. 116*

Dame un beso: Give me a kiss. *p. 101*

¿Dónde está Rita?: Where is Rita? *p. 110*

el amor: love *p. 108*

Es tarde: It's late. *p. 105*

es verdad: it's true *p. 132*

frijoles con tortillas y café: beans with tortillas and coffee *p. 100*

hijue puta: son of a whore *p. 112*

la abuela: the grandmother *p. 127*

la tía: the aunt *p. 103*

miedoso: timid person *p. 104*

Por favor, léame esto: Please, read this to me. *p. 108*

¿Qué dice?: What does it say? *p. 108*

qué lindo: how pretty *p. 107*

quizás: maybe *p. 104*

Rita bonita: lovely Rita *p. 101*

Virgen santísima: Blessed Virgin *p. 130*

una cervecita: a small beer *p. 106*

Section 4: Chapters 12–14

ayuntamiento: town hall   *p. 143*
¿Cuánto?: How much?   *p. 138*
el gobernador: the governor   *p. 143*
florecimiento: flowering; blossoming   *p. 156*
florecitas de papel: paper flowers   *p. 138*
Se murió: It died.   *p. 139*
¿Y su perro?: And your dog?   *p. 139*

Related Readings

CONTENTS

Night

by Louise Bogan

*The power of the sea pulses throughout
the lives of the villagers in the novel, for
the sea gives both life and death. At the
novel's conclusion, Remedios waits
patiently at the seashore, contemplating
the mysteries of life as the sun sets slowly.
In the following poem, the speaker reflects
upon the mysterious and powerful
rhythms of the sea.*

The cold remote islands
And the blue estuaries
Where what breathes, breathes
The restless wind of the inlets,
5 And what drinks, drinks
The incoming tide;

Where shell and weed
Wait upon the salt wash of the sea,
And the clear nights of stars
10 Swing their lights westward
To set behind the land;

Where the pulse clinging to the rocks
Renews itself forever;
Where, again on cloudless nights,
15 The water reflects
The firmament's partial setting;

—O remember
In your narrowing dark hours
That more things move
20 Than blood in the heart.

All day I hear the noise of waters

by James Joyce

*In the novel, the sea elicits many different
emotional states, from the patient
contemplation of Remedios to the frantic
terror of Chayo. As you read the following
poem by the Irish writer James Joyce, look
for evidence of the emotions that the
speaker associates with the sea.*

All day I hear the noise of waters
    Making moan,
Sad as the sea-bird is, when going
    Forth alone,
5 He hears the winds cry to the waters'
    Monotone.

The grey winds, the cold winds are blowing
    Where I go.
I hear the noise of many waters
10   Far below.
All day, all night, I hear them flowing
    To and fro.

Talking to the Dead
from Silent Dancing

by Judith Ortiz Cofer

*Judith Ortiz Cofer, a prominent contem-
porary writer, spent a good part of her
childhood in Puerto Rico. As she relates
in this autobiographical reminiscence, her
grandfather believed that he could
communicate with the spirit world, though
his practical wife remained unconvinced.
Cofer's grandfather, like Remedios in the
novel, used his spiritualist powers to help
those in need.*

My grandfather is a *Mesa Blanca* spiritist. This
means that he is able to communicate with the spirit
world. And since almost everyone has a request or
complaint to make from the *Other Side,* Papá once
was a much sought-after man in our pueblo. His
humble demeanor and gentle ways did much to
enhance his popularity with the refined matrons who
much preferred to consult him than the rowdy *santeros*
who, according to Papá, made a living through
spectacle and the devil's arts. *Santería,* like voodoo, has
its roots in African blood rites, which its devotees
practice with great fervor. *Espiritismo,* on the other
hand, entered the island via the middle classes who had
discovered it flourishing in Europe during the so-called
"crisis of faith" of the late nineteenth century. Poets
like Yeats belonged to societies whose members sought

answers in the invisible world. Papá, a poet and musician himself when he was not building houses, had the gift of clairvoyance, or *facultades,* as they are called in spiritism. It is not a free gift, however; being a spiritist medium requires living through *pruebas,* or tests of one's abilities.

Papá's most difficult *prueba* must have been living in the same house with Mamá, a practical woman who believed only in what her eyes recorded. If Papá's eyes were closed that meant that her lazy man was sleeping in the middle of the day again. His visionary states and his poetry writing were, I have heard, the primary reasons why Mamá had, early in their married life, decided that her husband should "wear the pants" in the family only in the literal sense of the expression. She considered him a "hopeless case," a label she attached to any family member whose drive and energy did not match her own. She never changed her mind about his poetry writing, which she believed was Papá's perdition, the thing that kept him from making a fortune, but she learned to respect his *facultades* after the one incident that she could not easily dismiss or explain.

Although Papá had been building a reputation for many years as an effective medium, his gifts had not changed his position in Mamá's household. He had, at a time determined by his wife, been banished to the back of the house to pursue his interests, and as for family politics, his position was one of quiet assent with his wife's wise decisions. He could have rebelled against this situation; in Puerto Rican society, the man is considered a small-letter god in his home. But, Papá, a gentle, scholarly man, preferred a laissez-faire approach. Mamá's ire could easily be avoided by keeping his books and his spiritist practice out of her sight. And he did make a decent living designing and building houses.

In his room at the back of the house he dreamt his dreams and interpreted them. There he also received the spiritually needy: the recent widows, the women who had lost children, and the old ones who had started making plans for the afterlife. The voices were kept low during these consultations. I know from having sat in the hallway outside his door as a child, listening as hard as I could for what I thought should be taking place—howlings of the possessed, furniture being thrown around by angry ghosts—ideas I had picked up from such movies as *Abbott and Costello Meet the Mummy,* and from misinterpreting the conversations of adults. But, Papá's seances were more like counseling sessions. Sometimes there were the sounds of a grown person sobbing—a frightening thing to a child—and then Papá's gentle, persuasive voice. Although most times I could not decipher the words, I recognized the tone of sympathy and support he was offering them. Two or more voices would at times join together in a chant. And the pungent odor of incense seeping through his closed door made my imagination quicken with visions of apparitions dancing above his table, waiting to speak through him to their loved ones. In a sort of trance myself, I would sometimes begin softly reciting an *Our Father,* responding automatically to the familiar experience of voices joined together in prayer and the church-smell of incense. What Papá performed in his room was a ceremony of healing. Whether he ever communicated with the dead I cannot say, but the spiritually wounded came to him and he tended to them and reassured them that death was not a permanent loss. He believed with all the passion of his poet's heart, and was able to convince others, that what awaits us all after the long day of our lives was a family reunion in God's extensive plantation. I believe he saw heaven as an island much like Puerto Rico, except without the inequities of backbreaking labor, loss and suffering which he could only justify to his followers as their prueba on this side of paradise.

Papá's greatest prueba came when his middle son, Hernán, disappeared. At the age of eighteen, Hernán had accepted a "free" ticket to the U.S. from a man recruiting laborers. It was a difficult time for the family, and reluctantly, Mamá had given Hernán permission to go. Papá, on the other hand, had uncharacteristically spoken out against the venture. He had had dreams, nightmares, in which he saw Hernán in prison, being tortured by hooded figures. Mamá dismissed his fears as fantasy-making, blaming Papá's premonitions on too much reading as usual. Hernán had been a wild teenager, and Mamá felt that it was time he became a working man. And so Hernán left the island, promising to write to his parents immediately, and was not heard from again for months.

Mamá went wild with worry. She imposed on friends and relatives, anyone who had a contact in the U.S., to join in the search for her son. She consulted with the police and with lawyers, and she even wrote to the governor, whose secretary wrote back that the recruiting of Puerto Rican laborers by mainland growers was being investigated by the authorities for the possibility of illegal practices. Mamá began to have nightmares herself in which she saw her son mistreated and worse. Papá stayed up with her during many of her desperate vigils. He said little, but kept his hands on his Bible, and would often seem to be speaking to himself in a trance. For once, Mamá did not ridicule him. She may have been too wrapped up in her despair. Then one night, Papá abruptly rose from his chair and rushed to his room where, with his carpenter's pencil, he began drawing something on the white cloth of his special table. Mamá followed him, thinking that her husband had gone mad with suffering for their child. But seeing the concentration on his face—it seemed to be lit with a light from within, she later told someone—she stood behind him for what seemed a long time. When he finished, he held a candle over the table and began explaining the picture as if to himself. "He is in a place far north. A place without a name. It is a place that can be found only by one who has been there. Here, there are growing things. Fruit, maybe. Sweet fruit. Not ready to be picked yet. There are lights in the distance. And a tall fence. Hernán sleeps here among the lights. He is dreaming of me tonight. He is lonely and afraid, but not sick or hurt."

Mamá began to see the things Papá described in the rough pencil lines on that tablecloth. Her mind turned into a map of memories, scraps of information, lines from letters she had received over the years, Christmas cards from strange places sent by a dozen nephews, or the sons of neighbors—young men for whom she had been a second mother—until she remembered this: a few years before Hernán's departure, Alicia's (Mamá's older sister) son, had also been "recruited" as a laborer. Like Hernán, he had not been informed as to exactly where he was going, only that it was in another Nueva York, not the city. Unlike her own son, her nephew had written home to say that he had been picking strawberries and did not like the job. Soon after, he had moved to a city near the farm where he had worked for a season. There he had married and settled down. Alicia would know the name of the place. But Papá had said it was a place without a name. Mamá decided to follow up on the only premonition she had ever allowed into her practical mind.

At that early hour, not quite dawn, the two of them set out for the country where Alicia lived; Papá was armed with his Bible and the symbol of his calling: a mahogany stick he had carved into a wand. Every spiritist must make one and take it with him on house calls. It is hollow and sometimes filled with Holy Water in order to keep "evil influences" at a distance, but Papá had put a handful of dirt from his birthplace in his, perhaps because his calling as a medium was more than anything a poet's choice of missions: a need to accept mortality while struggling for permanence. Anyway, that earth-filled stick was the only weapon I ever knew Papá to carry. That morning he and his wife walked together in silence, a rare occurrence: to Mamá, long silences were a vacuum her nature abhorred. They came home with hope in the form of a telephone number that day.

After sending for the high school English teacher to interpret, they called the city of Buffalo, New York. Mamá's nephew told them that he would start looking for Hernán at the farm right away. He said everyone just called it "the farm."

It turned out that Hernán was at the farm. The situation was very bad. The workers had been brought there by an unscrupulous farm worker who kept them (most of them very young and unable to speak English) ignorant as to their exact whereabouts. They lived in tents while they waited for the fruit to be ready for picking. Though they were given provisions, the cost was deducted from their paychecks, so by the time they were paid, their salary was already owed to the grower. The workers were told that mail was not picked up there and it would have to be taken to the nearest city after the harvest. Though Hernán and many of the other men protested their situation and threatened to strike, they knew that they were virtual prisoners and would have to wait for an opportunity to escape. Mamá's nephew had connections in Buffalo and was able to convince a social worker to accompany him to the farm where he found Hernán eager to lead the exodus. It was not as easy as that, though. Many days passed before an investigation was started which revealed the scheme behind the farm and many others like it based on the recruitment of young men under false pretenses. But Hernán had been found. And Mamá learned to respect, if not quite ever to publicly acknowledge, her husband's gift of clairvoyance.

She paid her tribute to him in her own way by embroidering a new cloth for his *mesa blanca* in a pattern based on his drawings of that night. She did it with white thread on white cloth, so that to see it one had to get very close to the design.

Paciencia

by Judith Ortiz Cofer

The woman described in the following poem has much in common with Remedios, the healer who plays such a key role in the novel.

The oldest woman in the village, Paciencia,
predicts the weather from the flight of birds:
Today, it will rain toads, she says,
squinting her face into a mystery of wrinkles
5   as she reads the sky—*tomorrow,*
it will be snakes.
                  Paciencia moves
with the grace of a ghost, walking unnoticed
down the roads lined with pleading eyes
10   and grasping hands, clothed in the invisibility
of her great age.
                Paciencia sucks the meat of figs
with toothless gums; sleeps little—shuffling
through empty rooms at night, making order,
15   breathing in the dust
careless youth stirs up in passing.
She hums as she weaves an endless pattern
of intersecting lines; she cocks her head sometimes,
as if listening for her name in the wind—
20   the dance of her bones evident through
      paper-thin skin
as she works—like a bird trapped in a sack.

And Paciencia does
what Paciencia pleases, having outlived rules.
She washes the limbs of the dead tenderly as babies
25 being readied for a nap; comforts the widows.
And while the world around her flames and freezes,
she tends the graves of the ones she remembers,
bending closer to the earth, like an old tree,
giving shelter, giving shade.

Death of a Young Son by Drowning

by Margaret Atwood

The speaker in this poem loses her young son in a tragic drowning accident, one similar to the drowning of Tonito in the novel. As you read the poem, compare the events and the speaker's feelings about her loss to Benítez's descriptions of Tonito's drowning and its effects on various characters.

He, who navigated with success
the dangerous river of his own birth
once more set forth

on a voyage of discovery
5   into the land I floated on
but could not touch to claim.

His feet slid on the bank,
the currents took him;
he swirled with ice and trees in the swollen
    water

10 and plunged into distant regions,
his head a bathysphere;
through his eyes' thin glass bubbles

he looked out, reckless adventurer
on a landscape stranger than Uranus
15   we have all been to and some remember.
There was an accident; the air locked,
he was hung in the river like a heart.
They retrieved the swamped body,

cairn of my plans and future charts,
20   with poles and hooks
from among the nudging logs.

It was spring, the sun kept shining, the new
   grass
lept to solidity;
my hands glistened with details.

25   After the long trip I was tired of waves.
My foot hit rock. The dreamed sails
collapsed, ragged.

               I planted him in this country
               like a flag.

Sophistication

by Sherwood Anderson

This short story is part of Winesburg, Ohio, *a famous collection of stories by American author Sherwood Anderson, first published in 1919. Like Benítez's novel, the collection portrays life in a small town and reveals the interconnected lives of the characters. In "Sophistication" the forces of fate and passion bring two characters together, a romance similar to that in the novel between Rafael, the teacher, and Esperanza, the midwife.*

It was early evening of a day in the late fall and the Winesburg County Fair had brought crowds of country people into town. The day had been clear and the night came on warm and pleasant. On the Trunion Pike, where the road after it left town stretched away between berry fields now covered with dry brown leaves, the dust from passing wagons arose in clouds. Children, curled into little balls, slept on the straw scattered on wagon beds. Their hair was full of dust and their fingers black and sticky. The dust rolled away over the fields and the departing sun set it ablaze with colors.

In the main street of Winesburg crowds filled the stores and the sidewalks. Night came on, horses whinnied, the clerks in the stores ran madly about, children became lost and cried lustily, an American town worked terribly at the task of amusing itself.

Pushing his way through the crowds in Main Street, young George Willard concealed himself in the stairway leading to Doctor Reefy's office and looked at the people. With feverish eyes he watched the faces drifting past under the store lights. Thoughts kept coming into his head and he did not want to think. He stamped impatiently on the wooden steps and looked sharply about. "Well, is she going to stay with him all day? Have I done all this waiting for nothing?" he muttered.

George Willard, the Ohio village boy, was fast growing into manhood and new thoughts had been coming into his mind. All that day, amid the jam of people at the Fair, he had gone about feeling lonely. He was about to leave Winesburg to go away to some city where he hoped to get work on a city newspaper and he felt grown up. The mood that had taken possession of him was a thing known to men and unknown to boys. He felt old and a little tired. Memories awoke in him. To his mind his new sense of maturity set him apart, made of him a half-tragic figure. He wanted someone to understand the feeling that had taken possession of him after his mother's death.

There is a time in the life of every boy when he for the first time takes the backward view of life. Perhaps that is the moment when he crosses the line into manhood. The boy is walking through the street of his town. He is thinking of the future and of the figure he will cut in the world. Ambitions and regrets awake within him. Suddenly something happens; he stops under a tree and waits as for a voice calling his name. Ghosts of old things creep into his consciousness; the voices outside of himself whisper a message concerning the limitations of life. From being quite sure of himself and his future he becomes not at all sure. If he be an imaginative boy a door is torn open and for the first time he looks out upon the world, seeing, as though they marched in procession before him, the countless figures of men who before his time have come out of nothingness into the world, lived their lives and again disappeared into nothingness. The sadness of sophistication has come to the boy. With a little gasp he sees himself as merely a leaf blown by the wind through the streets of his village. He knows that in spite of all the stout talk of his fellows he must live and die in uncertainty, a thing blown by the winds, a thing destined like corn to wilt in the sun. He shivers and looks eagerly about. The eighteen years he has lived seem but a moment, a breathing space in the long march of humanity. Already he hears death calling. With all his heart he wants to come close to some other human, touch someone with his hands, be touched by the hand of another. If he prefers that the other be a woman, that is because he believes that a woman will be gentle, that she will understand. He wants, most of all, understanding.

When the moment of sophistication came to George Willard his mind turned to Helen White, the Winesburg banker's daughter. Always he had been conscious of the girl growing into womanhood as he grew into manhood. Once on a summer night when he was eighteen, he had walked with her on a country road and in her presence had given way to an impulse to boast, to make himself appear big and significant in her eyes. Now he wanted to see her for another purpose. He wanted to tell her of the new impulses that had come to him. He had tried to make her think of him as a man when he knew nothing of manhood and now he wanted to be with her and to try to make her feel the change he believed had taken place in his nature.

As for Helen White, she also had come to a period of change. What George felt, she in her young woman's way felt also. She was no longer a girl and hungered to reach into the grace and beauty of womanhood. She had come home from Cleveland, where she was attending college, to spend a day at the Fair. She also had begun to have memories. During the day she sat in the grand-stand with a young man, one of the instructors from the college, who was a guest of her mother's. The young man was of a pedantic turn of mind and she felt at once he would not do for her purpose. At the Fair she was glad to be seen in his company as he was well dressed and a stranger. She knew that the fact of his presence would create an impression. During the day she was happy, but when night came on she began to grow restless. She wanted to drive the instructor away, to get out of his presence. While they sat together in the grand-stand and while the eyes of former schoolmates were upon them, she paid so much attention to her escort that he grew interested. "A scholar needs money. I should marry a woman with money," he mused.

Helen White was thinking of George Willard even as he wandered gloomily through the crowds thinking of her. She remembered the summer evening when they had walked together and wanted to walk with him again. She thought that the months she had spent in the city, the going to theaters and the seeing of great crowds wandering in lighted thoroughfares, had changed her profoundly. She wanted him to feel and be conscious of the change in her nature.

The summer evening together that had left its mark on the memory of both the young man and woman had, when looked at quite sensibly, been rather stupidly spent. They had walked out of town along a country road. Then they had stopped by a fence near a field of young corn and George had taken off his coat and let it hang on his arm. "Well, I've stayed here in Winesburg—yes—I've not yet gone away but I'm growing up," he had said. "I've been reading books and I've been thinking. I'm going to try to amount to something in life.

"Well," he explained, "that isn't the point. Perhaps I'd better quit talking."

The confused boy put his hand on the girl's arm. His voice trembled. The two started to walk back along the road toward town. In his desperation George boasted, "I'm going to be a big man, the biggest that ever lived here in Winesburg," he declared. "I want you to do something, I don't know what. Perhaps it is none of my business. I want you to try to be different from other women. You see the point. It's none of my business I tell you. I want you to be a beautiful woman. You see what I want."

The boy's voice failed and in silence the two came back into town and went along the street to Helen White's house. At the gate he tried to say something impressive. Speeches he had thought out came into his head, but they seemed utterly pointless. "I thought—I used to think—I had it in my mind you would marry Seth Richmond. Now I know you won't," was all he could find to say as she went through the gate and toward the door of her house.

On the warm fall evening as he stood in the stairway and looked at the crowd drifting through Main Street, George thought of the talk beside the field of young corn and was ashamed of the figure he had made of himself. In the street the people surged up and down like cattle confined in a pen. Buggies and wagons almost filled the narrow thoroughfare. A band played and small boys raced along the sidewalk, diving between the legs of men. Young men with shining red faces walked awkwardly about with girls on their arms. In a room above one of the stores, where a dance was to be held, the fiddlers tuned their instruments. The broken sounds floated down through an open window and out across the murmur of voices and the loud blare of the horns of the band. The medley of sounds got on young Willard's nerves.

Everywhere, on all sides, the sense of crowding, moving life closed in about him. He wanted to run away by himself and think. "If she wants to stay with that fellow she may. Why should I care? What difference does it make to me?" he growled and went along Main Street and through Hern's Grocery into a side street.

George felt so utterly lonely and dejected that he wanted to weep but pride made him walk rapidly along, swinging his arms. He came to Wesley Moyer's livery barn and stopped in the shadows to listen to a group of men who talked of a race Wesley's stallion, Tony Tip, had won at the Fair during the afternoon. A crowd had gathered in front of the barn and before the crowd walked Wesley, prancing up and down and boasting. He held a whip in his hand and kept tapping the ground. Little puffs of dust arose in the lamplight. "Hell, quit your talking," Wesley exclaimed. "I wasn't afraid, I knew I had 'em beat all the time. I wasn't afraid."

Ordinarily George Willard would have been intensely interested in the boasting of Moyer, the horseman. Now it made him angry. He turned and hurried away along the street. "Old windbag," he sputtered. "Why does he want to be bragging? Why don't he shut up?"

George went into a vacant lot and, as he hurried along, fell over a pile of rubbish. A nail protruding from an empty barrel tore his trousers. He sat down on the ground and swore. With a pin he mended the torn place and then arose and went on. "I'll go to Helen White's house, that's what I'll do. I'll walk right in. I'll say that I want to see her. I'll walk right in and sit down, that's what I'll do," he declared, climbing over a fence and beginning to run.

On the veranda of Banker White's house Helen was restless and distraught. The instructor sat between the mother and daughter. His talk wearied the girl. Although he had also been raised in an Ohio town, the instructor began to put on the airs of the city. He wanted to appear cosmopolitan. "I like the chance you have given me to study the background out of which most of our girls come," he declared. "It was good of you, Mrs. White, to have me down for the day." He turned to Helen and laughed. "Your life is still bound up with the life of this town?" he asked. "There are people here in whom you are interested?" To the girl his voice sounded pompous and heavy.

Helen arose and went into the house. At the door leading to a garden at the back she stopped and stood listening. Her mother began to talk. "There is no one here fit to associate with a girl of Helen's breeding," she said.

Helen ran down a flight of stairs at the back of the house and into the garden. In the darkness she stopped and stood trembling. It seemed to her that the world was full of meaningless people saying words. Afire with eagerness she ran through a garden gate and, turning a corner by the banker's barn, went into a little side street. "George! Where are you, George?" she cried, filled with nervous excitement. She stopped running, and leaned against a tree to laugh hysterically. Along the dark little street came George Willard, still saying words. "I'm going to walk right into her house. I'll go right in and sit down," he declared as he came up to her. He stopped and stared stupidly. "Come on," he said and took hold of her hand. With hanging heads they walked away along the street under the trees. Dry leaves rustled under foot. Now that he had found her George wondered what he had better do and say.

At the upper end of the Fair Ground, in Winesburg, there is a half decayed old grand-stand. It has never been painted and the boards are all warped out of shape. The Fair Ground stands on top of a low hill rising out of the valley of Wine Creek and from the grand-stand one can see at night, over a cornfield, the lights of the town reflected against the sky.

George and Helen climbed the hill to the Fair Ground, coming by the path past Waterworks Pond. The feeling of loneliness and isolation that had come to the young man in the crowded streets of his town was both broken and intensified by the presence of Helen. What he felt was reflected in her.

In youth there are always two forces fighting in people. The warm unthinking little animal struggles against the thing that reflects and remembers, and the older, the more sophisticated thing had possession of George Willard. Sensing his mood, Helen walked beside him filled with respect. When they got to the grand-stand they climbed up under the roof and sat down on one of the long bench-like seats.

There is something memorable in the experience to be had by going into a fair ground that stands at the edge of a Middle Western town on a night after the annual fair has been held. The sensation is one never to be forgotten. On all sides are ghosts, not of the dead, but of living people. Here, during the day just passed, have come the people pouring in from the town and the country around. Farmers with their wives and children and all the people from the hundreds of little frame houses have gathered within these board walls. Young girls have laughed and men with beards have talked of the affairs of their lives. The place has been filled to overflowing with life. It has itched and squirmed with life and now it is night and the life has all gone away. The silence is almost terrifying. One conceals oneself standing silently beside the trunk of a tree and what there is of a reflective tendency in his nature is intensified. One shudders at the thought of the meaninglessness of life while at the same instant, and if the people of the town are his people, one loves life so intensely that tears come into the eyes.

In the darkness under the roof of the grand-stand, George Willard sat beside Helen White and felt very keenly his own insignificance in the scheme of existence. Now that he had come out of town where the presence of the people stirring about, busy with a multitude of affairs, had been so irritating, the irritation was all gone. The presence of Helen renewed and refreshed him. It was as though her woman's hand was assisting him to make some minute readjustment of the machinery of his life. He began to think of the people in the town where he had always lived with something like reverence. He had reverence for Helen. He wanted to love and to be loved by her, but he did not want at the moment to be confused by her womanhood. In the darkness he took hold of her hand and when she crept close put a hand on her shoulder. A wind began to blow and he shivered. With all his strength he tried to hold and to understand the mood that had come upon him. In that high place in the darkness the two oddly sensitive human atoms held each other tightly and waited. In the mind of each was the same thought. "I have come to this lonely place and here is this other," was the substance of the thing felt.

In Winesburg the crowded day had run itself out into the long night of the late fall. Farm horses jogged away along lonely country roads pulling their portion of weary people. Clerks began to bring samples of goods in off the sidewalks and lock the doors of stores. In the Opera House a crowd had gathered to see a show and further down Main Street the fiddlers, their instruments tuned, sweated and worked to keep the feet of youth flying over a dance floor.

In the darkness in the grand-stand Helen White and George Willard remained silent. Now and then the spell that held them was broken and they turned and tried in the dim light to see into each other's eyes. They kissed but that impulse did not last. At the upper end of the Fair Ground a half dozen men worked over horses that had raced during the afternoon. The men had built a fire and were heating kettles of water. Only their legs could be seen as they passed back and forth in the light. When the wind blew the little flames of the fire danced crazily about.

George and Helen arose and walked away into the darkness. They went along a path past a field of corn that had not yet been cut. The wind whispered among the dry corn blades. For a moment during the walk back into town the spell that held them was broken. When they had come to the crest of Waterworks Hill they stopped by a tree and George again put his hands on the girl's shoulders. She embraced him eagerly and then again they drew quickly back from that impulse. They stopped kissing and stood a little apart. Mutual respect grew big in them. They were both embarrassed and to relieve their embarrassment dropped into the animalism of youth. They laughed and began to pull and haul at each other. In some way chastened and purified by the mood they had been in, they became, not man and woman, not boy and girl, but excited little animals.

It was so they went down the hill. In the darkness they played like two splendid young things in a young world. Once, running swiftly forward, Helen tripped George and he fell. He squirmed and shouted. Shaking with laughter, he rolled down the hill. Helen ran after him. For just a moment she stopped in the darkness. There is no way of knowing what woman's thoughts went through her mind but, when the bottom of the hill was reached and she came up to the boy, she took his arm and walked beside him in dignified silence. For some reason they could not have explained they had both got from their silent evening together the thing needed. Man or boy, woman or girl, they had for a moment taken hold of the thing that makes the mature life of men and women in the modern world possible.

An Astrologer's Day

by R. K. Narayan

In A Place Where the Sea Remembers, *two characters apparently possess spiritual powers. Remedios, the healer, uses her power to help others, while el brujo, the sorcerer, is willing to cast a spell of death if the price is right. In this story, by contrast, Narayan tells an amusing tale of an astrologer whose spiritual powers are a sham, though he proves himself to be a quick thinker.*

Punctually at midday he opened his bag and spread out his professional equipment, which consisted of a dozen cowrie shells, a square piece of cloth with obscure mystic charts on it, a notebook, and a bundle of palmyra writing. His forehead was resplendent with sacred ash and vermilion, and his eyes sparkled with a sharp abnormal gleam which was really an outcome of a continual searching look for customers, but which his simple clients took to be a prophetic light and felt comforted. The power of his eyes was considerably enhanced by their position—placed as they were between the painted forehead and the dark whiskers which streamed down his cheeks: even a half-wit's eyes would sparkle in such a setting. To crown the effect he wound a saffron-colored turban around his head. This color scheme never failed. People were attracted to him as bees are attracted to cosmos or dahlia stalks. He sat under the boughs of a spreading tamarind tree which flanked a path running through the town hall park. It was a remarkable place in many ways: a surging crowd was always moving up and down this narrow road morning till night. A variety of trades and occupations was represented all along its way: medicine sellers, sellers of stolen hardware and junk, magicians, and, above all, an auctioneer of cheap cloth, who created enough din all day to attract the whole town. Next to him in vociferousness came a vendor of fried groundnut, who gave his ware a fancy name each day, calling it "Bombay Ice Cream" one day, and on the next "Delhi Almond," and on the third "Raja's Delicacy," and so on and so forth, and people flocked to him. A considerable portion of this crowd dallied before the astrologer too. The astrologer transacted his business by the light of a flare which crackled and smoked up above the groundnut heap nearby. Half the enchantment of the place was due to the fact that it did not have the benefit of municipal lighting. The place was lit up by shop lights. One or two had hissing gaslights, some had naked flares stuck on poles, some were lit up by old cycle lamps, and one or two, like the astrologer's, managed without lights of their own. It was a bewildering crisscross of light rays and moving shadows. This suited the astrologer very well, for the simple reason that he had not in the least intended to be an astrologer when he began life; and he knew no more of what was going to happen to others than he knew what was going to happen to himself next minute. He was as much a stranger to the stars as were his innocent customers. Yet he said things which pleased and astonished everyone: that was more a matter of study, practice, and shrewd guesswork. All the same, it was as much an honest man's labor as any other, and he deserved the wages he carried home at the end of a day.

He had left his village without any previous thought or plan. If he had continued there he would have carried on the work of his forefathers—namely, tilling the land, living, marrying, and ripening in his cornfield and ancestral home. But that was not to be. He had to leave home without telling anyone, and he could not rest till he left it behind a couple of hundred miles. To a villager it is a great deal, as if an ocean flowed between.

He had a working analysis of mankind's troubles: marriage, money, and the tangles of human ties. Long practice had sharpened his perception. Within five minutes he understood what was wrong. He charged three paise per question, never opened his mouth till the other had spoken for at least ten minutes, which provided him enough stuff for a dozen answers and advices. When he told the person before him, gazing at his palm, "In many ways you are not getting the fullest results for your efforts," nine out of ten were disposed to agree with him. Or he questioned: "Is there any woman in your family, maybe even a distant relative, who is not well disposed towards you?" Or he gave an analysis of character: "Most of your troubles are due to your nature. How can you be otherwise with Saturn where he is? You have an impetuous nature and a rough exterior." This endeared him to their hearts immediately, for even the mildest of us loves to think that he has a forbidding exterior.

The nuts vendor blew out his flare and rose to go home. This was a signal for the astrologer to bundle up too, since it left him in darkness except for a little shaft of green light which strayed in from somewhere and touched the ground before him. He picked up his cowrie shells and paraphernalia and was putting them back into his bag when the green shaft of light was blotted out; he looked up and saw a man standing before him. He sensed a possible client and said, "You look so careworn. It will do you good to sit down for a while and chat with me." The other grumbled some reply vaguely. The astrologer pressed his invitation; whereupon the other thrust his palm under his nose, saying, "You call yourself an astrologer?" The astrologer felt challenged and said, tilting the other's palm towards the green shaft of light, "Yours is a nature . . ." "Oh, stop that," the other said. "Tell me something worthwhile. . . ."

Our friend felt piqued. "I charge only three paise per question, and what you get ought to be good enough for your money. . . ." At this the other withdrew his arm, took out an anna, and flung it out to him, saying, "I have some questions to ask. If I prove you are bluffing, you must return that anna to me with interest."

"If you find my answers satisfactory, will you give me five rupees?"

"No."

"Or will you give me eight annas?"

"All right, provided you give me twice as much if you are wrong," said the stranger. This pact was accepted after a little further argument. The astrologer sent up a prayer to heaven as the other lit a cheroot. The astrologer caught a glimpse of his face by the match light. There was a pause as cars hooted on the road, jutka drivers swore at their horses, and the babble of the crowd agitated the semidarkness of the park. The other sat down, sucking his cheroot, puffing out, sat there ruthlessly. The astrologer felt very uncomfortable. "Here, take your anna back. I am not used to such challenges. It is late for me today. . . ." He made preparations to bundle up. The other held his wrist and said, "You can't get out of it now. You dragged me in while I was passing." The astrologer shivered in his grip; and his voice shook and became faint. "Leave me today. I will speak to you tomorrow." The other thrust his palm in his face and said, "Challenge is challenge. Go on." The astrologer proceeded with his throat drying up, "There is a woman . . ."

"Stop," said the other. "I don't want all that. Shall I succeed in my present search or not? Answer this and go. Otherwise I will not let you go till you disgorge all your coins." The astrologer muttered a few incantations and replied, "All right. I will speak. But will you give me a rupee if what I say is convincing? Otherwise I will not open my mouth, and you may do what you like." After a good deal of haggling the other agreed. The astrologer said, "You were left for dead. Am I right?"

"Ah, tell me more."

"A knife has passed through you once?" said the astrologer.

"Good fellow!" He bared his chest to show the scar. "What else?"

"And then you were pushed into a well nearby in the field. You were left for dead."

"I should have been dead if some passerby had not chanced to peep into the well," exclaimed the other, overwhelmed by enthusiasm. "When shall I get at him?" he asked, clenching his fist.

"In the next world," answered the astrologer. "He died four months ago in a far-off town. You will never see any more of him." The other groaned on hearing it. The astrologer proceeded:

"Guru Nayak—"

"You know my name!" the other said, taken aback.

"As I know all other things. Guru Nayak, listen carefully to what I have to say. Your village is two days' journey due north of this town. Take the next train and begone. I see once again great danger to your life if you go from home." He took out a pinch of sacred ash and held it to him. "Rub it on your forehead and go home. Never travel southward again, and you will live to be a hundred."

"Why should I leave home again?" the other said reflectively. "I was only going away now and then to look for him and to choke out his life if I met him." He shook his head regretfully. "He has escaped my hands. I hope at least he died as he deserved." "Yes," said the astrologer. "He was crushed under a lorry." The other looked gratified to hear it.

The place was deserted by the time the astrologer picked up his articles and put them into his bag. The green shaft was also gone, leaving the place in darkness and silence. The stranger had gone off into the night, after giving the astrologer a handful of coins.

It was nearly midnight when the astrologer reached home. His wife was waiting for him at the door and demanded an explanation. He flung the coins at her and said, "Count them. One man gave all that."

"Twelve and a half annas," she said, counting. She was overjoyed. "I can buy some jaggery and coconut tomorrow. The child has been asking for sweets for so many days now. I will prepare some nice stuff for her."

"The swine has cheated me! He promised me a rupee," said the astrologer. She looked up at him. "You look worried. What is wrong?"

"Nothing."

After dinner, sitting on the pyol, he told her, "Do you know a great load is gone from me today? I thought I had the blood of a man on my hands all these years. That was the reason why I ran away from home, settled here, and married you. He is alive."

She gasped. "You tried to kill!"

"Yes, in our village, when I was a silly youngster. We drank, gambled, and quarreled badly one day— why think of it now? Time to sleep," he said, yawning, and stretched himself on the pyol.

Acknowledgments

(continued from page ii)

Oxford University Press Canada: "Death of a young son by drowning," from *The Journals of Susanna Moodie* by Margaret Atwood. Copyright © 1970 by Oxford University Press Canada. Reprinted by permission of Oxford University Press Canada.

Viking Penguin: "An Astrologer's Day," from *Malgudi Days* by R. K. Narayan. Copyright © 1982 by R. K. Narayan. Used by permission of Viking Penguin, a division of Penguin Books USA Inc.